...AS I FOLLOW

CHRIST

Also by Dwain Esmond:

Beyond the In-a-Pinch God
Can You Hear Me Now?
24-7-365: One Year in the Word

To order, **call 1-800-765-6955.**

Visit us at **www.reviewandherald.com**
for information on other Review and Herald® products.

DWAIN N. ESMOND, EDITOR

...AS I FOLLOW CHRIST

THE 20 ESSENTIALS EVERY LEADER SHOULD KNOW

REVIEW AND HERALD® PUBLISHING ASSOCIATION
Since 1861 | www.reviewandherald.com

Review and Herald® titles may be purchased in bulk for educational, business, fund-raising, or sales promotional use. For information, e-mail SpecialMarkets@reviewandherald.com.

The Review and Herald® Publishing Association publishes biblically based materials for spiritual, physical, and mental growth and Christian discipleship.

The editor assumes full responsibility for the accuracy of all facts and quotations as cited in this book.

Statements in this volume attributed to other speakers/writers are included for the value of the individual statements only. No endorsement of those speakers'/writers' other works or statements is intended or implied.

Scripture quotations marked ESV are from *The Holy Bible*, English Standard Version, copyright © 2001 by Crossway Bibles, a division of Good News Publishers. Used by permission. All rights reserved.

Texts credited to Message are from *The Message*. Copyright © 1993, 1994, 1995, 1996, 2000, 2001, 2002. Used by permission of NavPress Publishing Group.

Scripture quotations marked NASB are from the *New American Standard Bible,* copyright © 1960, 1962, 1963, 1968, 1971, 1972, 1973, 1975, 1977, 1995 by The Lockman Foundation. Used by permission.

Texts credited to NIV are from the *Holy Bible, New International Version.* Copyright 1973, 1978, 1984, 2011 by Biblica, Inc. Used by permission. All rights reserved worldwide.

Texts credited to NKJV are from the New King James Version. Copyright © 1979, 1980, 1982 by Thomas Nelson, Inc. Used by permission. All rights reserved.

Scripture quotations marked NLT are taken from the *Holy Bible,* New Living Translation, copyright © 1996, 2004, 2007 by Tyndale House Foundation. Used by permission of Tyndale House Publishers, Inc., Carol Stream, Illinois 60188. All rights reserved.

Bible texts credited to NRSV are from the New Revised Standard Version of the Bible, copyright © 1989 by the Division of Christian Education of the National Council of the Churches of Christ in the U.S.A. Used by permission.

This book was
Edited by Gerald Wheeler
Copyedited by Jocelyn Fay
Interior designed by Derek Knecht / Review & Herald® Design Center
Cover design by Mark Bond
Typeset: Minion Pro 11/13

PRINTED IN U.S.A.

17 16 15 14 13   5 4 3 2 1

Library of Congress Cataloging-in-Publication Data

As I follow Christ : the 20 essentials every leader should know / Dwain Esmond, editor.
    pages cm
1. Christian leadership—Seventh-Day Adventists. I. Esmond, Dwain, 1971-   , editor of compilation.
  BV652.1.A8 2013
  253—dc23
                        2012051777

ISBN 978-0-8280-2724-3

DEDICATION

To Harper and Clarissa Esmond,
who led me to Christ.

CONTENTS

Introduction

When my colleague Howard Scoggins, marketing vice president for Review and Herald Publishing Association, approached me about doing a book on leadership, my first thought was probably the same one that whipsawed through your mind when you saw this book: *Please. Not another book on leadership!* With a glut of leadership books dotting the publishing landscape, your disgust at the sight of another is understandable.

Few leadership texts today are as enduring as Alfred Lansing's *Endurance: Shackleton's Incredible Voyage,* published in 1959. This tale of Sir Earnest Shackleton's ill-fated 1914 voyage through the Antarctic remains a staple of business school case studies to this day. In more recent times, has any book on leadership done more for management literature than *Team of Rivals,* the groundbreaking biography of Abraham Lincoln by historian Doris Kearns Goodwin? It boasts a cult following that includes, most notably, President Barack Obama, who credits it with shaping his governing philosophy. *Lincoln,* director Steven Spielberg's much-acclaimed docudrama, was based in part on Goodwin's tome. Measured against Lansing's *Shackleton* or Goodwin's *Lincoln,* most leadership books fall flat.

Yet there remains one book that is the best text ever written on the subject of leadership. Care to guess what it is?

Crack any of its 66 books, and you are sure to find someone taking a stand, leading a band, building a brand, or lending a hand. Look closely and you will find no shortage of heroes and winners, or louts and losers, for that matter. Some morally ambidextrous figures have managed to don both capes in a single lifetime. The Bible's rich tapestry of noble and ignoble human endeavor yields countless pearls of wisdom for the attentive leader.

The conviction that Scripture furnishes eternal principles of leadership that every leader should know is the foundation of this book. More specifically, we believe the life of Jesus Christ offers a treasure trove of management insight that millions have found indispensable to the task of leading. *As I Follow Christ* seeks to distill some of the Bible's guidance on leadership into 20 essentials that every leader should know.

In these pages you will find practical principles that can be applied immediately to your leadership context. You will learn what God looks for in a leader, how He sets them up, what He does when they fall, as some inevitably do. You will hear the call to courageous leadership, and the Spirit's whisper to tend carefully your inner life. You will be summoned to the heights of excellence in your professional life and home life. In short, this book will both challenge and equip you to be a better leader—God's leader.

My hope is that through these pages you will be led to God and that He will lead others through you.

In the Master's service,
Dwain N. Esmond, general editor
Vice President, Editorial Services
Review and Herald Publishing Association

Chapter 1

THE LEADER GOD SEEKS

Cindy Tutsch
FORMER ASSOCIATE DIRECTOR, ELLEN G. WHITE ESTATE

Tsunamis, earthquakes, floods, hurricanes, tornadoes, economic meltdowns, governments collapsing—all fill the headlines day after day. As our world undergoes increasing chaos, people everywhere are looking for leaders to make sense of it all, to put everything back "to rights." Have you ever thought that God too is seeking leaders through whom He can work to bring hope and the good news to a panicked and terrified planet?

Maybe you are saying, "Don't look at me, Lord!" But if you are a Christian, you are a leader. Part of our leadership responsibility is to use our influence to lead others to follow and trust Jesus. We do so in different ways, according to our spiritual gifts. Some of us may be administrators or executives, many of us are parents, others are teachers, some are vision casters, and still others have extraordinary talents for hospitality, praying, or fixing things. But unless you've been living in an isolated cave for the past 10 years and have seen no one during that time, you have a life filled with people. Whatever your sphere of influence—be it family, classroom, community, local workplace, or even a global arena—knowing what God is looking for in leadership will help you make a bigger impact on those around you.

Driven in part by the cataclysmic events striking the world around them, people are searching for spirituality and meaning in life—but often on dead-end streets. God has created us with a desire to know Him, but hordes of humans attempt to find connection and relationship through mysticism, channeling, or Eastern religions—or through alcohol, mind-altering drugs, and sexual promiscuity.

Yet God's desire is still to restore in humankind His own image, thus enabling the Godhead to have intimate companionship and communication with Their created beings. Such a deep level of relationship includes humanity's grateful obedience to God as a response to His love and grace. And the primary means through which God presently communicates love and grace, as well as His will for individuals, is through the Holy Spirit.

The Spirit works through various agencies: Scripture, impressions on the heart tested by His Word, the book of nature, extrabiblical prophets, and the community of faith. In this chapter let's look at the Spirit-inspired qualifications for leadership we find in Scripture and the writings of Ellen White.

In times of crisis, calamity, or deliverance, God declares His intentions for humanity through His chosen leader. Thus Noah announced earth's impending destruction by the global deluge, Moses proclaimed deliverance of God's people from the Egyptians, Jeremiah and Isaiah warned of national calamity, and John the Baptist heralded the arrival of the Messiah. Seventh-day Adventists believe the destruction of our planet followed by the second coming of Jesus is imminent. In this end-time of earth's history God is looking for leaders to declare the messages of Revelation 14: God's judgment has come, Babylon is fallen, and those who honor all of God's commandments will not receive the catastrophic mark of the beast.

Those three angels of Revelation 14 represent us—you and me![1] Our most important leadership task is to help everyone—our families, our communities, all of earth's inhabitants—understand the urgency of our times and our need to choose, know, and serve God. How do we become the quality of leader that God can use for such a mind-boggling task? Let me suggest seven ways:

1. **Spend time in prayer.** Oh, not just a quick prayer with our hand on the doorknob on the way to our fast life. I mean earnest, committed, intense prayer. Fasting and prayer. Nights of prayer. That's how Jesus received power for leadership, and so must we (see 1 Thess. 5:17; Luke 11:9).[2]
2. **Receive the Holy Spirit.** Without the gift of God's Spirit to call us to confession and repentance, give us wisdom and insight, and energize our witness, *our leadership will fail* (see Acts 1:4, 5, 8; John 14:26).[3]
3. **Know God's Word.** Through immersing ourselves in Scripture we come to know God. As we respond to that growing understanding, He gradually changes us to become like Him. It is a divine miracle

of epic proportions, and there simply are no shortcuts. Whatever it takes, whatever you have to cut out of your life, spend *time* communing with God in His Word (see John 5:39; 2 Tim. 3:14-17).[4]

4. **Care for those who are poor.** Does this one surprise you? Actually, Scripture has hundreds of references to caring for those who have the least in society. As a person provides for the needs of the poor, he or she develops the kind of compassionate character that God desires every leader to demonstrate (see Ps. 41:1; Matt. 25:31-46).[5]

5. **Exercise self-control.** Through Christ you can curb your temper, your appetite, and your complaining. Rehearse your blessings continually, and look for the good in others (see Gal. 5:22, 23; Prov. 16:32).[6]

6. **Depend on God.** The more responsibilities you find yourself called to bear, the greater is the temptation to trust in yourself and your own abilities. Remember the biblical story of Mary and Martha? Jesus affirmed Mary's decision to sit in His presence and learn from Him (see Prov. 3:5-7; Matt. 11:29).[7]

7. **Learn from your mistakes.** Only Jesus is the perfect leader. The rest of us will goof up sometimes. God lets us to learn and grow from our failures, and we must allow similar development in others (see 1 Peter 5:6; Matt. 18:23-35).[8]

Do you feel a little overwhelmed by what seem impossibly high ideals? Don't despair! God is eager to help you (Phil. 4:13). His eye roams through the earth (Zech. 4:10), looking for people—just like you—through whom He can accomplish His compassionate purposes. If you long to influence people within your particular family or community context to know, understand, and love God, He will hone your leadership skills.

And remember, God doesn't always call the qualified, but He is always willing to qualify the called![9]

---

[1] Ellen G. White, *Testimonies for the Church* (Mountain View, Calif.: Pacific Press Pub. Assn., 1948), vol. 5, pp. 455, 456.

[2] See also Ellen G. White, *Gospel Workers* (Washington, D.C.: Review and Herald Pub. Assn., 1915), p. 100; Ellen G. White, *Counsels to Parents, Teachers, and Students* (Mountain View, Calif.: Pacific Press Pub. Assn., 1913), p. 323.

[3] See also Ellen G. White, *The Desire of Ages* (Mountain View, Calif.: Pacific Press Pub. Assn., 1898), p. 672; E. G. White, *Testimonies,* vol. 6, p. 322.

[4] See also Ellen G. White, *The Great Controversy* (Mountain View, Calif.: Pacific Press Pub. Assn., 1911), pp. 513-602; E. G. White, *Counsels to Parents, Teachers, and Students*, pp. 428, 429.

[5] See also Ellen G. White, *Christ's Object Lessons* (Washington, D.C.: Review and Herald Pub. Assn., 1900), pp. 382-387; E. G. White, *Testimonies*, vol. 2, p. 24.

[6] See also Ellen G. White, *Patriarchs and Prophets* (Mountain View, Calif.: Pacific Press Pub. Assn., 1890), p. 421; Ellen G. White, *Counsels on Diet and Foods* (Washington, D.C.: Review and Herald Pub. Assn., 1938), p. 59.

[7] See also Ellen G. White, *Prophets and Kings* (Mountain View, Calif.: Pacific Press Pub. Assn., 1917), pp. 30-32; E. G. White, *Testimonies*, vol. 9, p. 282.

[8] See also Ellen G. White, *Testimonies to Ministers and Gospel Workers* (Mountain View, Calif.: Pacific Press Pub. Assn., 1923), p. 304; E. G. White, *Testimonies*, vol. 3, p. 495.

[9] A portion of this chapter is adapted from *Ellen White on Leadership: Guidance for Those Who Influence Others* (Nampa, Idaho: Pacific Press Pub. Assn., 2008).

Chapter 2

THE LEADER'S SPIRITUAL LIFE

Ted N. C. Wilson
PRESIDENT, GENERAL CONFERENCE OF SEVENTH-DAY ADVENTISTS

It is not easy to be a church administrator today as we face the end of time and the challenges that come with it. To carry out your work and mission according to God's direction takes a strong spiritual connection with Him. It is essential that you maintain such a close relationship with Him, not only since you need to perform your responsibilities well, but also since God wants to bless others through the Holy Spirit's work in you and through you.

Seventh-day Adventists have long believed in and promoted a balanced approach to life that includes the mental, social, physical, and spiritual aspects of our existence. They will affect every element of your life as a spiritual administrator and must be regulated by your connection with heaven and your adherence to the spiritual and natural laws given by the Lord.

You determine your spirituality by how you allow God to control your life and bring biblical principles into your everyday work and personal experiences. The principle of Micah 6:8 must permeate your thinking and actions: "He has shown you, O man, what is good; and what does the Lord require of you but to do justly, to love mercy, and to walk humbly with your God?" (NKJV). If you will fulfill the three requirements God outlines, you will be a powerful spiritual administrator and exhibit a strong spiritual life. God asks you to do that which is right or just and not to shirk your duty in fulfilling the law through His power. However, you are not to be so rigid in your justice that you forget to apply mercy, as appropriate, through the leading of the Holy Spirit.

In addition, God requires you to be humble in your approach to Him and your fellow human beings. When you "walk humbly with your God," you will naturally do the same with others. You will realize that you do not have all the answers and that only in relying totally on Christ can you effectively lead people in a spiritual way.

As you fulfill Micah 6:8, through God's direct leading in your life, you will exhibit the spiritual life that Paul portrays in Colossians 1:9-18 that has Christ in everything you do. Paul says, "For this reason we also, since the day we heard it, do not cease to pray for you, and to ask that you may be filled with the knowledge of His will in all wisdom and spiritual understanding; that you may walk worthy of the Lord, fully pleasing Him, being fruitful in every good work and increasing in the knowledge of God; strengthened with all might, according to His glorious power, for all patience and longsuffering with joy; giving thanks to the Father who has qualified us to be partakers of the inheritance of the saints in the light. He has delivered us from the power of darkness and conveyed us into the kingdom of the Son of His love, in whom we have redemption through His blood, the forgiveness of sins. He is the image of the invisible God, the firstborn over all creation. For by Him all things were created that are in heaven and that are on earth, visible and invisible, whether thrones or dominions or principalities or powers. All things were created through Him and for Him. And He is before all things, and in Him all things consist. And He is the head of the body, the church, who is the beginning, the firstborn from the dead, that in all things He may have the preeminence" (NKJV).

In order for you to be a spiritual administrator, you must understand that Christ "is the head of the body" and has preeminence in all things. When you respond in humble respect to our Creator, who brought us and our world into existence in six literal, consecutive, 24-hour days of recent origin, and you accept Him as the Lord of your life because He justified you through His death on the cross and now daily sanctifies you through the indwelling of the Holy Spirit, He can then use you in a powerful way as a spiritual administrator.

The connection with Christ in all you do will have a powerful effect on your influence. The following areas especially shape the spiritual life of an administrator:

1. **Study and have a literal belief in the Word of God.** You must daily take time to study the Bible and allow the Word to soak into your very being to show yourself approved before God as 2 Timothy 2:15 indicates. Your understanding and belief in the Bible must involve

a literal acceptance of what it says. Our church has long held to the historical-grammatical method of interpreting Scripture through allowing the Bible to interpret itself—line upon line, precept upon precept. However, one of the most sinister attacks against the Bible and its doctrines comes from those who believe in the historical-critical method of explaining the Bible—individuals influenced by the unbiblical approach of "higher criticism" that is a deadly enemy of our theology and mission. Such an approach puts a scholar or individual above Scripture and gives inappropriate license to decide what he or she perceives as truth based on the resources and education of the critic. Stay away from this type of approach. It does not lead people to trust God and His Word and will destroy correct theology and mission. So preach the Word as we are admonished in 2 Timothy 4:2.

2. **Support the 28 fundamental beliefs of the Seventh-day Adventist Church.** Have complete trust in and belief of the 28 fundamental beliefs of the church. Know them and realize they are based on the Word of God. Teach them to others and promote them. They are biblical beliefs. Feed God's sheep the Word of God as indicated in John 21:16.

3. **Have complete trust in and study the Spirit of Prophecy.** Accept the writings of Ellen G. White as one of God's greatest gifts to His remnant people, the Seventh-day Adventist Church. Her works have counsel for just about every aspect of the Christian life and are just as relevant today as when first written. They are messages from heaven. Read them daily. Accept, promote, teach, and support her writings. Believe the biblical instruction about the Spirit of Prophecy in Revelation 12:17 and 19:10.

4. **Have an active prayer life.** As an administrator you cannot survive without a constant personal prayer life that puts you in contact with the heavenly source of all wisdom and guidance. Pray in the morning, at noon, at night . . . all the time. Ask the Lord for guidance as you counsel people, chair a committee, give instruction for a project, deal with problems, and as you conduct every activity of the day. Without such a prayer life you will not be a spiritual administrator or have the success God wishes for your work. Believe fully the admonition in 1 Thessalonians 5:17 to pray without ceasing.

5. **Seek revival and reformation.** Recognize that we are truly in a Laodicean setting and need revival and reformation through the power of the Holy Spirit. Be willing to humble yourself before God and ask your fellow officers and colleagues to do the same as you seek the power of the latter rain through the Holy Spirit. Realize that we are at the end of time and desperately need the Lord to remake us in His image to transform both our own lives and the church. Let Revelation 3:18-20 be fulfilled in your life so that you will allow Christ to come into your own heart.

6. **Share your faith.** Be willing to let the Holy Spirit use you as you personally share your faith with those you meet. Doing so will strengthen your spiritual life. Be willing to hold public evangelistic meetings that will not only bring others to a knowledge of Christ and decision for Him, but will increase your own belief in this great Advent movement and our fundamental beliefs. Fulfill the Great Commission of Matthew 28:19, 20.

7. **Lift up Christ, His righteousness, and the sanctuary service.** In your daily personal and work activities make Christ the focus of your life. Speak often of Him to others. Help your associates and those you come in contact with to realize that only through Christ's ministry during His life, His death on the cross at Calvary, and His ministry as our High Priest in the heavenly sanctuary (as outlined in Daniel 8:14 and the book of Hebrews) can we have full assurance of eternal life. We owe everything to Christ for justification, sanctification, and ultimately glorification. Let your message flow from your personal relationship with Him and what Peter indicates in 1 Peter 1:17-21.

8. **Proclaim the three angels' messages.** Enthusiastically and confidently spread the three angels' messages of Revelation 14:6-12. Realize that God has given the Seventh-day Adventist Church a unique message for the world, and that we are to present it through the Holy Spirit's power.

9. **Have a sunny disposition and be a unifier.** Be positive in your approach to life and encourage others, always being part of the solution and not part of the problem. Fulfill Christ's prayer of unity found in John 17. Follow the counsel in 2 Corinthians 5:18, 19 to bring reconciliation to those around you.

10. **Be observant and affirming.** In your relationships with others,

always be aware of their activities and accomplishments. When they have been working hard and have accomplished certain goals, express your appreciation, thereby encouraging them to do more for the Lord. Remember that you are all part of the Lord's team. Be a fulfillment of Proverbs 15:23 with a word spoken in due season.

11. **Have a deep trust in God's leading.** Do not doubt for a moment that God is leading the Seventh-day Adventist Church. It is not just another denomination but a mighty movement of the Lord. Have an abiding trust in the promises of the Scriptures and writings of Ellen G. White. God will carry His people through to the culmination of the Great Commission given to His people. God has called the Seventh-day Adventist Church for a unique role of proclaiming the three angels' messages, and it will continue to the end of time in its special role of lifting up the true worship of God. We find the characteristics of God's last-day church identified in Revelation 12:17 and Revelation 14:12.

12. **Adopt physical exercise and proper eating habits.** Realize that what you eat and drink and how you conduct your physical life (exercise, sleep, rest, recreation) will greatly affect your spiritual life. The moral and natural laws have a close relationship, since God Himself gave all of them. Take time for proper physical exercise and appropriate rest. Do not wear yourself out. If you do, you will be hurting your spiritual life as well. Eat a good vegetarian diet and avoid all harmful beverages and other detrimental habits. God will honor you as He did Daniel. Follow the counsel in 3 John 2 so that you have good spiritual and physical health.

13. **Be fair and balanced.** In your dealings with people be known as someone who is fair and balanced in the way you handle situations. Evaluate situations carefully and impartially. Make reasonable decisions based on principles and counsel from the Bible and Ellen G. White. Let Philippians 4:8 guide your thinking and decision-making.

14. **Be a good listener.** A spiritual administrator will learn the art of listening, reserving comments until after having heard the "whole" story. Don't jump to conclusions. Wait and listen. Be willing to learn. It is better to have fewer words said and more time spent listening. Fulfill Proverbs 1:5, which indicates that as wise individuals listen carefully they will learn and grow in understanding.

15. **Seek counsel from others.** In your work as a spiritual administrator, ask for advice and input from other godly people. Do not think you know all the answers. Constantly seek guidance and instruction from those who know the Lord and whom you trust. Proverbs 11:14 reminds us that safety resides in a multitude of counselors.

16. **Stand for the right.** Be willing to support what is right "though the heavens fall," as the book *Education* says.[1] Do not fear to take a stand for something, even if it is not popular. Allow the Holy Spirit to lead you in forming your opinion and beliefs. Let the Word of God and the writings of Ellen G. White open to you understanding of the principles of the matter under discussion. Be respectful and honorable as you share what you believe is an appropriate position. Through God's guidance, you too can say what is found in Joshua 24:15: "As for me and my house, we will serve the Lord" (NKJV).

17. **Stand for those who cannot stand.** Be willing to support individuals or causes that have no voice but need to be heard. God will give you guidance as you help those who have little or no access to decision-making. The Lord asks you to be the voice of the widow and the orphan and others in need. Follow the ministry of Christ in Luke 4:18.

18. **Ask for wisdom every day.** Every morning, claim James 1:5, pleading for divine wisdom for your daily duties. Realize that you are powerless without complete direction from the Lord. God will give you what you need to accomplish your tasks in being a spiritual administrator.

19. **Be a humble servant.** In all your dealings with others remember that you are God's servant. Allow Micah 6:8 to rule your actions. Remember Proverbs 15:33, which says that "before honour is humility." Fulfill Christ's instruction in Matthew 20:26-28 that whoever would be chief should be a servant. Let us follow His example. Accept Proverbs 3:7, which tells us, "Do not be wise in your own eyes; fear the Lord and depart from evil" (NKJV).

20. **Believe that Christ's coming will be soon.** Accept and believe in the promises and prophecies that indicate Christ's second coming is imminent. Greater and greater signs indicate that His return is near. Shape your thinking and actions in accordance with this impelling belief that we are living in the last days of earth's history. Speak about Christ's coming and preach about it.

Realize that the descriptions of Christ's return in Matthew 24 and 2 Peter 3 are accurate and true. Believe with certainty the words of Christ recorded in Revelation 22:7: "Behold, I am coming quickly!"(NKJV).

As a Seventh-day Adventist administrator seeking to increase your spiritual connection with heaven for a more effective work at the end of time, commit yourself to following Proverbs 3:5, 6, which urges us to "trust in the Lord with all your heart, and lean not on your own understanding; in all your ways acknowledge Him, and He shall direct your paths" (NKJV).

Realize that a leader's spiritual life must flow out of a deep relationship with Christ and a complete dependence on the power of the Holy Spirit.

In *Selected Messages* we read, "We must have a greater nearness to God. Much less of self and much more of Jesus Christ and His grace must be brought into our everyday life."[2]

As our spiritual connection increases, we will more and more realize our need of Christ. We will understand that our greatest requirement as spiritual administrators is to plead with God for revival and reformation in our lives and that of His church. More and more we will grasp what Ellen G. White tells us in *Selected Messages*: "A revival of true godliness among us is the greatest and most urgent of all our needs. To seek this should be our first work."[3] As we come to the end of time, may we truly be God's agents, nurturing the revival and reformation through the power of the Holy Spirit that will bring the latter rain and the coming of the Lord.

Always, as spiritual administrators for God's church and His people, we should ponder and incorporate the divine counsel through Peter in 1 Peter 1:13-21: "Therefore gird up the loins of your mind, be sober, and rest your hope fully upon the grace that is to be brought to you at the revelation of Jesus Christ; as obedient children, not conforming yourselves to the former lusts, as in your ignorance; but as He who called you is holy, you also be holy in all your conduct, because it is written, 'Be holy, for I am holy.' And if you call on the Father, who without partiality judges according to each one's work, conduct yourselves throughout the time of your stay here in fear; knowing that you were not redeemed with corruptible things, like silver or gold, from your aimless conduct received by tradition from your fathers, but with the precious blood of Christ, as of a lamb without blemish and without spot. He indeed was foreordained before the foundation of the world, but was manifest in these last times for you who through Him believe in God, who raised Him from the dead and gave Him glory, so that your faith and hope are in God" (NKJV).

May your spiritual life as an administrator or other leader constantly increase as you plead with the Lord for revival, reformation, and the latter rain of the Holy Spirit. And may your hope grow as you lean completely on Christ, who bought you with His precious blood and intercedes for you in the Most Holy Place in preparation for His glorious return to take us home to heaven. Even so, come, Lord Jesus.

---

[1] Ellen G. White, *Education* (Mountain View, Calif.: Pacific Press Pub. Assn., 1903), p. 57.

[2] Ellen G. White, *Selected Messages* (Washington, D.C.: Review and Herald Pub. Assn., 1958, 1980), book 2, p. 376.

[3] *Ibid.,* book 1, p. 121.

Chapter 3

THE LEADER AS SERVANT

Sung Kwon

DIRECTOR, ADVENTIST COMMUNITY SERVICES, NORTH AMERICAN DIVISION

W e often encounter the three most fundamental questions of life: Who am I? Where did I come from? What is my destiny?

Which question is most important? The key question is the second one: Where did I come from? Depending on your answer, your destiny will be changed.

God says that we are a chosen people, a royal priesthood, a holy nation, a people belonging to God (1 Peter 2:9). Therefore, the most essential question is not who we are in this life, but to whom we belong and whose we are. This, in fact, will determine who we are.

We witness the life of Christ at the cross of Calvary—the grand monument of mercy and regeneration, salvation and redemption—when the Son of God was uplifted on the cross.[1] Ellen G. White says, "The sacrifice of Christ as an atonement for sin is the great truth around which all other truths cluster. In order to be rightly understood and appreciated, every truth in the Word of God, from Genesis to Revelation, must be studied in the light that streams from the cross of Calvary."[2] The cross of Calvary is crucial to Christians not only for His death and resurrection, which are the core values of the plan of salvation, but more so for how He lived his life—not just how He died, but how He lived. As His children and the disciples of our Lord Jesus Christ, this is the life we must follow.

Jesus lived His life as a humble servant: "Just as the Son of Man did not come to be served, but to serve, and to give his life as a ransom for many" (Matt. 20:28, NIV). Therefore, the bottom line of the Christian journey is to be servants of God. Our ambition is not leadership but servanthood, leading servants into servanthood of leadership. Servanthood is the Christian journey. It is saying we are following Jesus all the way as true disciples, and it is foundational and central to the Christian's life and ministry. Being leading servants is serving *with* Jesus, not just *for* Jesus. Jesus said, "Whoever wants to be my disiple must deny themselves and take up their cross daily and follow me" (Luke 9:23, NIV).

Servanthood is an essential requirement for a leader. God gave various spiritual gifts to the church—disciples, prophets, teachers, ministers, etc.— and regardless of each individual's calling, servanthood is the basis for all gifts that encourages others to serve, to give, to help, to be merciful and hospitable. These traits are even more critical in the church than in the corporate world. As our Lord Jesus Christ served, so ought we to serve one another.[3]

However, we have some challenges. One of them is that we don't want to be a servant—we want to be leaders. Rick Warren says, "Thousands of books have been written on leadership, but few on servanthood. Everyone wants to lead; no one wants to be a servant. We would rather be generals than privates. Even Christians want to be 'servant-leaders,' not just plain servants. But to be like Jesus is to be a servant."[4] Robert Banks says, "Leadership is the key term and servant is the qualifier. What we need today is not, as is so often suggested, more servant leaders, but properly understood, more leading servants."[5] We need more *leading servants* who understand that: the gospel must be preached, the lost must be found, the believers must be equipped, the poor must be served, the lonely must be enfolded into community, and God gets the credit for it all.[6] Ellen G. White says that "kneeling in faith at the [foot of the] cross, he has reached the highest place to which man can attain."[7] The highest place is not being a director, president, or CEO—it is the foot of the cross.

If one does not have a servant's heart and a servant's attitude, it is possible to serve in church for a lifetime without ever being a servant. "Leaders who are not real servants first with a servant's heart are potentially dangerous. They tend to abuse power and pamper their egos."[8] They care only to maximize their pleasure and minimize their pain, and usually end up exercising a leadership style and approach that can be destructive to them and their followers.

The leader must serve the organization and its members. Ask yourself, Do I think more about others than about myself? Do I base my identity in Christ? Do I think of ministry as an opportunity, not an obligation? Christian servanthood is not only serving Jesus but serving *with* Jesus. It involves not only being servants of Christ but being servants *with* Christ.

Throughout Jesus' ministry we witness a genuine servanthood approach toward humanity, especially people who were marginalized, disadvantaged, and disenfranchised from society. They were the poor, the sick, the unclean, all shunned as sinful people. Jesus expanded the kingdom of God to places, people, and cultures that the Jews had never considered God to be interested in.[9]

Jesus grieved over the multitudes of people who were helpless, and brought hope to their lives by ministering according to their needs. Through this compassionate service opportunity Jesus was able to build a trust relationship. "Christ's method alone will give true success in reaching the people. The Savior *mingled* with men as one who *desired* their good. He *showed* His sympathy for them, *ministered* to their needs, and *won* their confidence. Then He bade them, 'Follow Me.'"[10] Jesus mingled with people, identified their needs, met their needs, and developed a trust relationship. And then He said to the people, "Follow Me."

The purpose of being a disciple is not only to proclaim the good news, the word of salvation, but also to demonstrate the love of God to people who are in need. "It is God himself who has made us what we are and given us new lives from Christ Jesus; and long ages ago he planned that we should spend these lives in helping others" (Eph. 2:10, TLB). This is why service is not an option in Christian servanthood. We are called to maintain and improve social conditions of society. We are commanded to create kingdom values in this world. We are commissioned to become change-makers in our communities.

However, in their institutional preoccupation, some churches have abandoned their real identity and reason for existence. Like the Sadducees, who were in charge of the Jerusalem's Temple-based activity and sold out to materialism and religious ritual, they become systematic and mechanical religious practitioners. Like the Pharisees, who were holding control in the synagogues and dominating the religious agenda, policies, and operational procedures, they produced a dead religion.

The reality is that in general people in the community don't care much about organized religious institutions or club memberships. They think that religious people do not see people; they see only causes, behaviors, and stereotypes. And most of them think religious people do not feel emotionally with their hearts but rather think and process logically.[11]

In Korea we say father's love is logical and a mother's love is emotional. When my son was younger, he would fall and hurt himself often. When he was hurt, my wife ran after him to see if he was OK, and to make sure there were no broken bones. On the other hand, I, his father, behaved logically. I watched from a distance, analyzing the circumstances. Then I'd approach him and ask him why he had fallen, how he fell, and what he had learned from the experience. While the boy is crying out loud for a hug, I am trying to figure out why! Sometimes we do that as a church. People are crying out for the love of God, forgiveness, and assurance of God's grace and mercy, while we are trying to figure out why and how they fell.

There are times we Christians are great at speaking the truth without love. We have the truth and know what people desperately need, but the challenge is that people will not receive it from us because we haven't earned the privilege to share it.

Anatole France said, "The average man, who does not know what to do with his life, wants another one which will last forever." When was the last time you thought, *How do I turn myself into a missionary? How do I deploy myself as a missionary in a community transformation?* Since we are called into the servanthood of Christianity, we ought to take the gospel to the marketplace. Jesus went to the places where the people were. Likewise, we need churches where people are—at the mall, supermarkets, and coffee shops. For the most part, people are not coming to us—we have to go to them. Being a servant requires that we continually adopt new ways of thinking and working.

As leading servants are we making any impact on the communities in which our institutions are located? What about our churches, schools, and hospitals? Are they better places to live because of our existence in these communities? When was the last time that you heard someone from the community say, "I am a better father today because of your church"; "I am a better mother because of your hospital"; or "I am a better person because of your school"? The challenge is *not* about our ability to do this—it is about our *pride* and *our lack of concern for people.* That is what God is concerned about. Because of corporate "churchianity" we are often reluctant to be connected with people outside the church. Mother Teresa said, "You can find Calcutta all over the world, if you have eyes to see." We see people in need everywhere, but the challenge is that we don't see God's people; we see stereotypes, cause, and external appearances. We need to pray for God's vision in our lives, to see His people with faces of God's image.

There are times that we have been taught and trained to sell our brand of religion. We are so intent on convincing people that their lives are screwed up, their faith is wrong, and their beliefs are incorrect that we overlook the fact that we are unskilled at listening to and engaging people.[12] We often look at them as *prospects* for membership rather than as spiritual beings with the same quest for God that we have. We need to stop training people as mechanics to work within the church industry and instead equip and develop them to become disciples for the kingdom of God as leading servants to turn the world upside down (Acts 17:6). We need to shift from *doing* church at the clubhouse to *being* church in the world.

We must pray for God's intervention in our lives and listen to people's struggles and challenges, looking for an opportunity to serve and demonstrate the love of God. When we intentionally and sincerely approach people who are disfranchised, disassociated, and marginalized in our communities, we will witness changes in their lives—and changes in our communities. Again, the challenge is not about individual *ability,* but about *availability.*

Adapting and extending the works of Burns[13] and of Kouzes and Posner[14] examined the leader behaviors associated with servant leadership and identified five exemplary practices through their research. These learnable servant leadership practices include:

1. **Model the way.** The ability to establish principles as to how goals will be attained and ways individuals interact, characterized by role-modeling appropriate behavior and setting expectations.
2. **Inspire a shared vision.** The ability to envision, passionately communicate, and enlist support for future possibilities for organizations and groups.
3. **Challenge the process.** A willingness to examine and change that status quo, characterized by informed risk-taking and a willingness to learn from mistakes.
4. **Enable others to act.** The capacity to engage others in shared processes, characterized by mutual processes, characterized by mutual investment, collaboration, and empowerment.
5. **Encourage the heart.** The capacity to recognize and celebrate individual and group accomplishments. This practice can serve as a powerful personal learning tool and find a new expression in this emerging world. We must become leading servants as Christian disciples, who order their lives around missionary purpose and who believe they are responsible for fulfilling the Great Commission. Their organizational chart is not hierarchical but rather a flat circle. They measure their effectiveness and impact of ministry beyond the four walls of the church, asking: How is our dependability—are we doing what we say we will do? How is our timeliness—are we doing it when we say we will do it? How is our

empathy—are we doing it with an eye to the needs of community? How is our tangible evidence—are we doing it in ways that lets communities know a service has been performed?

As we serve the community through Christ's love and faith in action, Christians will demonstrate what it means to be a leading servant, and we will begin to knock down the barriers between churches and communities at large. This is why the community outreach is both proclaiming the good news, as well as demonstrating God's love and concern for every soul.

The bottom line is that we are called to servanthood in discipleship. When we say we are Christians, we are not talking about *self-serving* Christianity, but *serving* Christianity—serving disciples.[15]

God has called us to servanthood; this is nonnegotiable. We follow Jesus in humble and loving servanthood, as He Himself was the humble servant. By Christ's model of compassionate service and love, we can lead others to the kingdom.

---

[1] See Michael S. Horton, *The Kingdom and the Church* (Grand Rapids: Zondervan, 2012).

[2] E. G. White, *Gospel Workers*, p. 315.

[3] See Siang-Yang Tan, *Full Service: Moving From Self-serve Christianity to Total Servanthood* (Grand Rapids: Baker Books, 2006).

[4] Rick Warren, *The Purpose Driven Life: What on Earth Am I Here For?* (Grand Rapids: Zondervan, 2012), p. 329.

[5] In Tan, p. 55.

[6] See Richard Stearns, *The Hole in Our Gospel: What Does God Expect of Us?* (Nashville: Thomas Nelson, 2009).

[7] Ellen G. White, *The Acts of the Apostles* (Mountain View, Calif.: Pacific Press Pub. Assn., 1911), p. 210.

[8] Tan, p. 56.

[9] See Harvie M. Conn and Manuel Ortiz, *Urban Ministry: The Kingdom, the City and the People of God* (Downer's Grove, Ill.: IVP Academic, 2010).

[10] Ellen G. White, *The Ministry of Healing* (Mountain View, Calif.: Pacific Press. Pub. Assn., 1905), p. 143. (Italics supplied.)

[11] See Ronald J. Sider, Philip N. Olson, and Heidi Rolland Unruh, *Churches That Make a Difference: Reaching Your Community With Good News and Good Works* (Grand Rapids: Baker Books, 2002).

[12] See Ted Kluck and Kevin DeYoung, *Why We Love the Church: In Praise of Institutions and Organized Religion* (Chicago: Moody Publishers, 2009).

[13] See James MacGregor Burns, *Leadership* (New York: Harper & Row, 1978).

[14] See James M. Kouzes and Barry Z. Posner, *The Leadership Challenge: How to Get Extraordinary Things Done in Organization* (San Francisco: Jossey-Bass, 1987), pp. 30-35; idem, *The Leadership Challenge: The Most Trusted Source on Becoming a Better Leader* (San Francisco: Jossey-Bass/Pfeiffer, 2007).

[15] See Philip Jenkins, *The Next Christendom: The Coming of Global Christianity* (New York: Oxford University Press, 2011).

Chapter 4

CALLED TO LEAD

David Smith

SENIOR PASTOR, COLLEGEDALE SEVENTH-DAY ADVENTIST CHURCH, TENNESSEE

He walked into the dining hall, his military uniform the only clue that he was a hero. His gaunt look, thin body, awkward gait, and indirect gaze belied the deeds he had done on the battlefield. As a child, I could not understand how Desmond Doss had done anything significant. Humility marked him. I recall holding his medals in my hand and wondering what he had done to earn them.

Years later I read a book about Desmond Doss and learned how God had taken a shy boy from Georgia and empowered him to risk his life repeatedly in order to save many soldiers from certain death. It wasn't Doss's courage that struck me or his winning of the Congressional Medal of Honor. Rather, his humility and absolute dedication to God most caught my attention.

It is interesting that in his book *Good to Great* Jim Collins describes leaders of highly effective companies who are similar to Desmond Doss. They reflect a combination of humility, dedication, and perseverance. Collins devotes an entire chapter of his book to illustrating and describing such individuals, whom he terms level 5 leaders. According to Collins, a level 5 leader is "an individual who blends extreme personal humility with intense professional will."[1] Such leaders are ambitious for their institutions, not themselves. Unselfishly they promote the greater good and serve a high purpose.

While Collins admits that the humility and selflessness of level 5 leaders surprised him, these traits mark the people whom God calls to lead. Often the Lord selects individuals who appear unsuited for the leadership task to which He summons them. Consider the calling of Jeremiah. In Jeremiah 1:4-10 we read: "The word of the Lord came to me, saying, 'Before I formed you in the womb I knew you, before you were born I set you apart; I appointed you as a prophet to the nations'" (verse 5, NIV). Jeremiah's response reveals his misgivings about his suitability for the role to which God had appointed him. "'Alas, Sovereign Lord,' I said, 'I do not know how to speak; I am too young'" (verse 6, NIV). God tells him that he doesn't need to fear, because He will provide whatever Jeremiah needs to function as a prophet.

From Jeremiah's account we can see that the subject of divine calling is complex. The Lord knew what the prophet would do before his birth, yet Jeremiah was unaware of God's plan until the Lord revealed it. Calling is something we discover, not something we know from birth. God discloses it in His time and way. It may be, as in Jeremiah's case, seemingly mismatched to our strengths or gifts.

Why does God's calling so often surprise us? One reason is that He delights in asking people to do what He, not they, can do so that their humility will contribute all the more glory to Him and to the furtherance of His work on earth. Consider Paul's observation in 1 Corinthians 1: "Brothers and sisters, think of what you were when you were called. Not many of you were wise by human standards; not many were influential; not many were of noble birth. But God chose the foolish things of the world to shame the wise; God chose the weak things of the world to shame the strong" (verses 26, 27, NIV). Why did God do this? "So that no one may boast before him" (verse 29, NIV). A few chapters later the apostle declared: "I am the least of the apostles and do not even deserve to be called an apostle, because I persecuted the church of God. But by the grace of God I am what I am" (1 Cor. 15:9, 10, NIV).

By God's grace we are what we are. That was the case with one of my wife's uncles, Robert Boothby. He was convicted that God wanted him to be an evangelist despite his severe stutter. As he progressed through school, his professors encouraged him to consider another vocation. It seemed inconceivable that this humble man could present an evangelistic sermon without embarrassing himself and distracting his audience. But Robert Boothby persisted. God had clearly spoken to him and called him to be an evangelist.

When Pastor Boothby began to speak at his first evangelistic tent meeting, the most remarkable thing happened. While he gave his sermon, he did not stutter. Thanks to the work of the Holy Spirit, he spoke with eloquence and power. When the sermon ended, his stuttering returned.

The pattern repeated itself throughout his highly successful evangelistic career. Many became part of the heavenly kingdom because a humble man was willing to be a leader for God.

Many years ago Haddon Robinson, in a sermon on Jeremiah 1, observed that "we often hear people say, 'God has called me to do such and such.' And we often ask, 'What does it mean to be called by God?' It is not the whole answer, but it is a necessary part of the answer to say that being called by God involves a feeling and a fear that God wants you to do a task for Him that very few can do. Not that you are better than others, or worthy to do the task, or especially qualified to do it, or even want to do it; but that God wants you to do it and will make up for your deficiencies."

So the Lord's call for us as leaders may not always be what we would choose for ourselves. It may not always bring us recognition or success as judged by others. But nothing is more satisfying in life than doing what God has summoned you to do. And if you partner with Him to do His will for your life, remarkable things can happen.

I was reminded of this when I returned for my 20-year reunion to the boarding academy I attended. As part of the reunion experience, my classmates sat around a circle and shared highlights of the past two decades in our lives. By worldly standards our class was a resounding success. Many of us were professionals with advanced degrees. Unabashedly we shared our accomplishments, family information, and significant contributions to society. With each testimony we basked in an aura of achievement.

The last person to speak was Tom, one of the most likable class members.[2] Though he struggled with stuttering, we all loved him. When we were in school, he was always so accepting and supportive. We wondered what great thing had he done since then.

Speaking warmly, he congratulated all of us on our success. "Imagine!" he said. "Who would have predicted 20 years ago that we would have accomplished all that we have?" We nodded in agreement. He told us he was proud of our degrees, awards, houses, cars, and all the things we had shared to signify our success.

Then he paused, looked at us seriously, and stated, "But you can have your cars, your houses, your awards, your accomplishments, your degrees. If you don't have Jesus Christ as your Lord and Savior, you have nothing. Please, I beg you, give your lives to Jesus Christ. That is what counts most."

The room was suddenly quiet. We all looked down at the floor. All but one of us. One brave classmate, realizing that Tom was the only class member who had not related anything about himself, asked, "What do you do? What have you accomplished in the past 20 years? You haven't told us."

Tom smiled. "I'm a dentist," he said. We quietly laughed. With his stuttering, how could he be a dentist? "Seriously, what do you do?" the classmate persisted.

"I'm a dentist." Then he recounted going through college, convicted that God wanted him to enter that profession. He described his experiences in dental school, listening to the pleas of his professors to consider another occupation. Surely no one would be comfortable being a patient of a stuttering dentist.

But Tom was convinced that even though he too could not understand how he could be a successful dentist, God wanted him to be one. So he graduated from dental school, opened up a brand-new practice, and experienced a miracle. No, he did not stop stuttering. Instead, his testimony was that when patients entered his waiting room, the Holy Spirit was present to put them at ease. His patients were perfectly comfortable even though he stuttered, and he had a thriving practice.

Tom is a level 5 leader. Not needing credit or recognition for what he does, he depends solely on God to accomplish for him what he cannot do for himself. The result is a remarkable witness for the Lord.

God needs more leaders like Desmond Doss and Tom. He seeks humble men and women willing to respond to His call regardless of their circumstances. The Lord wants those who revel more in the glory God receives for what they do than for the recognition they gain.

If God has called you to lead, trust Him. Don't focus on your inadequacy or fears. Concentrate on His all-sufficiency. Do what He asks you to do. If you do, your leadership will provide Him with a unique and powerful way to serve others. Nothing is more satisfying in leadership than partnering with God to accomplish His will, all for His glory and honor. So be a leader for God and watch what the Lord will do.

---

[1] Jim Collins, *Good to Great* (New York: HarperCollins, 2001), p. 21.

[2] Not his real name.

Chapter 5

The Leader's Family

Willie and Elaine Oliver

*Directors, Department of Family Ministries,
General Conference of Seventh-day Adventists*

By the end of our first year of marriage things were not going too well. As a young pastor in the Bronx—one of the boroughs of New York City—I (Willie) was committed to leading the congregation assigned to my care with a spiritual maturity representative of the gospel of Jesus Christ.

While fond of my preacher husband, I (Elaine) was a young professional who, after earning a bachelor's degree in business and accounting, then getting married, then spending a year working on Wall Street, had just landed a job at one of the most prestigious women's colleges in the eastern United States. The work was challenging and the environment invigorating. And yes, I was very busy with my own life.

To get started in pastoral ministry I (Willie) had earned a bachelor's degree in theology and a master's degree in religion in the area of pastoral counseling, with concentrations in marriage and family counseling. As a pastor's son I had experienced firsthand my parents' ministry of helping families stay together. On many occasions I engaged Dad in conversation about the challenges in relationships and the importance of having a strong and healthy family life. Invariably he declared that success in life as a whole had a lot to do with being effective in one's personal family life.

We were madly in love with each other, really loved Jesus, and assumed that our marriage was as strong as an ox. After all, we grew up in Adventist homes—although very different in configuration—attended Adventist schools, and were now a young pastoral couple leading a relatively small inner-city church to be light and salt in the community in which it existed. What could possibly go wrong with our marriage?

The truth is, as we often share with audiences around the world, all marriages will naturally move toward a state of alienation. That happens because we are human, and "all have sinned and fall short of the glory of God" (Rom. 3:23, NKJV). There are no perfect marriages and families because there are no perfect people. For any marriage to remain viable the partners must be intentional about connecting with each other through the power and grace of God. That foundation is essential to nurture a healthy family.

So regardless of our leadership positions, we found ourselves drifting away from each other—despite our love for each other, love for God, and love for the work we were doing on behalf of God and the church.

A few years later, when our marriage had found deeper satisfaction and stability, we hosted our first marriage retreat. I (Willie) was director of family ministries for the Greater New York Conference. By this time I (Elaine) had received a promotion to the Ivy League university across the street from the women's college where I had been working. We were now parents of two young children. During the retreat our facilitators, Lennox and Ouida Westney, from Silver Spring, Maryland, engaged us in dialogue.

During our conversation I (Willie) confessed to Elaine that I had prayed to God to help me solve our marital problems. My request was that if He would simply allow Elaine to go to sleep until resurrection morning things would work out much better for me. Please, I requested, allow her no pain or blood.

My (Willie's) appeal to God was that the tension and feelings of resentment taking place in our marriage were not what I had signed up for, and He couldn't possibly want a leader in His church to be going through all the pressure I was experiencing at home. God knew that as a church leader I would not divorce my wife. And, after all, what we were experiencing in marriage—I conjectured in my state of frustration—was the fault of the conference leaders and other more seasoned pastors who had invariably dropped hints about my need to get married. God must have been sending a different message, but the *brethren* pushed me in this direction. After all, one of the conference administrators had asked me in front of Elaine, just a week after we started dating, "Do you think you can get this young woman to marry you?" And I fell for the trick and answered in my most confident voice, "I think so." Surely it was a ploy of Satan. But God would help me— so I argued with myself.

Since God promises to give us His peace (John 14:27) and supply all our needs (Phil. 4:19), I (Willie) knew He would be reasonable enough to provide me a new, more amenable and more compatible spouse who would make my life happy, thus enabling me to serve more effectively in the ministry He had called me to. It is amazing what kind of conversations we think we can have with God when life takes strange turns because of poor choices we make when relating to our spouse. Incredible suspense filled me as I waited for a response from Elaine.

I (Elaine) began to smile. I could see the expression on his face, not sure what to expect from me. So I shared with him my side of the same story. "You know, it's funny," I said. "I prayed the exact same prayer."

The tension suddenly left the room. We laughed, looked at each other knowingly, and joined the other couples regrouping to continue listening to the biblical wisdom being presented by our guest presenters.

The truth is, being in a position of leadership is not an inoculation against the rigors embedded in family life. Rather, it is often a barrier to stronger and healthier family relationships. The Bible is filled with examples of exactly that problem.

As people in leadership, we are passionate and driven about our responsibilities. After all, God called us to make a difference, and we have committed ourselves to accomplishing that task in an outstanding way. Such determination is typically so strong that no one needs to encourage or persuade us to do our *jobs* well. We just do. It is the reason others often notice our potential and invite us to even greater leadership opportunities.

What happens to leaders, though, is that we often lack healthy boundaries to manage our families and work so that both can fully benefit. We cannot easily turn off the passion and drive that we have for our calling when we get home. Although we love our spouse and children, we at the same time believe that the important work we are doing simply cannot wait. And with technology today making us available to anyone at any time, we must be disciplined or pay a heavy price. Such a reality often gets magnified for Christian leaders, because, after all, we are doing *God's work,* and nothing is more important than *that.* Or is it?

In our quest to be fully committed to the mission of the church, generations of church leaders have passed on the message to younger leaders that dedicated leadership means being on the job 24/7. Now, that may sound good and may feed our longing to be needed, but it is not compatible with the message in Scripture or the writings of Ellen G. White.

Ellen White declares: "Nothing can excuse the minister for neglecting the inner circle for the larger circle outside. The spiritual welfare of his family comes first."[1] We cannot escape that responsibility by trying to find the right spouse who can then step into the family gap created by our heavy leadership demands. While every leader needs a committed and gifted spouse to help shoulder the responsibilities of life, Ellen White warns us here that no level of dedication to the work of ministry can ever excuse the demise of our families.

Ellen White also offers: "One well-ordered, well-disciplined family tells more in behalf of Christianity than all the sermons that can be preached."[2] If that is true, and we believe it is, then we must reexamine our family relationships and do what must happen every time we confront truth we are not practicing—alter our ways to give honor and glory to God.

To be sure, nothing will change unless we shift the paradigm that informs the way we live. Stephen R. Covey suggests that "most people feel there's a real gap between what really matters most to them—including family—and the way they live their daily lives."[3] So the issue is not our extrinsic lack of commitment but rather the absence of any corresponding behavior that demonstrates that our families are really a top priority to us.

The apostle Paul shares his struggles with not following through with what he believes in, when he states: "The good that I will to do, I do not do; but the evil I will not to do, that I practice. . . . O wretched man that I am! Who will deliver me from this body of death? I thank God—through Jesus Christ our Lord!" (Rom. 7:19-25, NKJV).

As Christian leaders like Paul, our advantage is having full access to the power of God. We must identify what needs to change about the way we do family, then do whatever is necessary. But it is not something we can do by ourselves. We must be willing to avail ourselves of the help of a professional Christian counselor—one of the gifts of the Spirit God has given (1 Cor. 12:1-11) for the edification of the church.

During our certification as facilitators of Covey's *The 7 Habits of Highly Effective Families*, we learned that to reprioritize our families it is necessary to employ the basic change model, also known as the see, do, get model. Essentially, we need to *see* things differently, in order to *do* things differently, so that we can *get* a different result. In short, we need to *see* our families as most important, to *do* things that convey our regard for and value of them, and then we will *get* stronger and healthier family relationships.

If the counsel to have well-ordered, well-disciplined families to accomplish more on behalf of the gospel is really true, then we must live our lives as leaders based on the values of the kingdom of God. Paul reinforces this notion in 1 Corinthians 10:31: "Whether you eat or drink, or whatever you do, do all to the glory of God" (NKJV).

Unless we do more to be intentional about connecting with our spouse and children every day, our relationships will naturally drift toward a state of alienation. And if that happens, we will not be able to fulfill the leadership potential God wants us to achieve.

A large body of marriage and family research literature suggests that most relationships experience distress because of a lack of effective communication. If married people, and people in general, learned to communicate better, they would have much more understanding between them and a basis for a stronger and healthier relationship.[4]

One of our favorite passages in the Bible states: "A word fitly spoken is like apples of gold in settings of silver" (Prov. 25:11, NKJV). The verse suggests that God wants us to use words—that is, when we speak to our respective families—as if giving a precious gift. There is never a bad time to receive a gift of golden apples in a frame of silver. If the words we employ with our loved ones were as precious as the gift mentioned above, their tone and message would increase the regard and appreciation we have for each other.

Mark and Debra Laaser suggest that we are all born with seven basic desires that must be met for us to feel fulfilled in life. The first desire the Laasers propose is that of being heard and understood.[5] The Bible affirms this concept by declaring in James 1:19: "This you know, my beloved brethren. But everyone must be quick to hear, slow to speak and slow to anger" (NASB). The truth is that we will be able to hear and understand another human being, particularly members of our family, only when we apply this verse to heart.

In addition to speaking kindly in our families, becoming good listeners is a wonderful and essential quality for superior family relationships. Most difficulties in the family will worsen when we fail to listen to each other. And that includes parents listening to their children. As you can see, the Bible text shared above states that "everyone must be quick to hear." Everyone includes parents, husbands, wives, and whoever else is a part of a household. Failure to listen leads to lack of understanding and alienation. Listening to our spouse, and especially our children and other family members, will convey attention, respect, regard, and deep love to them. Scripture observes that "love will cover a multitude of sins" (1 Peter 4:8, NKJV).

To be able to live happy lives (a prerequisite to being most productive), it is crucial to be proactive—which means living within our circle of control. Rather than being reactive—in which we simply respond in conversation based on our emotions or by the first thing that naturally comes out of our mouths—we pause (pray), think, and carefully choose a reply that takes into consideration the future viability of our family relationships. On this note Ellen White declares: "If impatient words are spoken to you, never reply in the same spirit."[6]

Leadership has its privileges and challenges. One of the most significant trials—yet simultaneously an immense honor—is to have a family. We know there are no perfect families, because there are no perfect people. Still, it is our responsibility to understand the place our families must have in the hierarchy of our priorities and be faithful to that privilege even more so than to our passion for the leadership role that God has called us to.

Be of good courage and make the paradigm shift to see your family members differently, so that your behavior toward them will be transformed and you will get a superior response that will expand your leadership capacity.

---

[1] E. G. White, *Gospel Workers*, p. 204.

[2] Ellen G. White, *The Adventist Home* (Nashville: Southern Pub. Assn., 1952), p. 32.

[3] Stephen R. Covey, *The 7 Habits of Highly Effective Families* (New York: Golden Books, 1997), p. 115.

[4] Howard J. Markman, Scott M. Stanley, and Susan L. Blumberg, *Fighting for Your Marriage* (San Francisco: Jossey-Bass, 2001), p. 4.

[5] Mark and Debra Laaser, *The Seven Secrets of Every Heart* (Grand Rapids: Zonderman Pub. House, 2008), p. 15.

[6] E. G. White, *The Ministry of Healing*, p. 486.

Chapter 6

God's Woman as Leader

Prudence LaBeach Pollard
*Assistant Vice President for Faculty
Development, Leadership, and Research, Oakwood University*

Introduction

God's call to leadership (Matt. 28:18-20; Acts 1:21, 22) embraces the mutuality of male and female believers. Jesus describes leadership in the community of believers not as a position but rather as a process. It is the result of the exercise of our spiritual gifts and talents. Our gifts of service influence those served. And the unambiguous purpose of our service is to share the gospel with nonbelievers and to minister to fellow believers. Thus disciples are leaders, and they exercise leadership[1] in response to His call. As apostles, the disciples accepted the divine commission to teach and lead others to Him. In both Scripture and in the life and teachings of Jesus we see an emphasis on the influence-building behaviors of believers and not on position or status as a requirement for teaching about the kingdom of heaven. Jesus calls all to Christian leadership, whether Jew or Gentile, rich or poor, man or woman, child or adult, Pharisee or publican (Gal. 3:26-28), because leadership is the exercise of influence for the advancement of God's kingdom.

Women Lead Differently Than Their Male Counterparts: Fact or Fiction?

Here is a fact that we know: *When men and women are granted full personhood, respected for their gifts, aptitudes, and talents, they will follow those gifts into professions that utilize their talents and maximize their sense of fulfillment.* Men and women are biologically different, yet mutually reflective of the image of God. For the Christian the concept of biological and gender differences should not be surprising. In Genesis 1:27, 28 we find

39

a description of God's complementary creation of humanity as one of "male and female." Both male and female are wholly capable of rationality and functionality, of independent thought and actions. Yet in the interaction between male and female we see a higher order of living, one of relationality. Thus the challenge of interacting with others who are recognizably different refines our ability to understand, to communicate with, and possibly to care about the other person. Differences and independence are evident, but interdependence is best understood through a study of our foreparents, Adam and Eve. And it was dependence on God and interdependence that were tested when Satan tempted them to disobey God's command. Sadly, Adam and Eve failed the *interdependence test* when they exerted their independence. They blamed each other rather than demonstrating other-centeredness. Our differences are evident and function as a dominant characteristic of our individuality. In fact, independence does not require careful thought. But interdependence, the other-centeredness present in the transformed character, originates from the relational aspect of our humanity and is visible only when we are considerate of another. Christians call it love.[2]

The shared image of God that Adam and Eve together possessed provides Christians with a clear understanding of the mutuality within the two aspects of our humanity. We see differences in the biological features and physiological functions of men and women, in their psychological makeup, and in their observable behaviors. Such differences result from both nature and nurture. And it is also nurture that shapes how we relate to those differences and evaluate them as "good" or "bad."

Some cultures regard difference as a negative. But Scripture makes no room for preferring one gender over the other. Still, certain cultures select male babies over female ones, view females as the weaker sex, and regard them as vulnerable and needing to be covered up and cloistered. However, other cultures celebrate infants regardless of their sex, view men and women as equally capable, and expect men and women to refrain from sexual violence against each other and hold them responsible for their sexual behavior. God Himself established difference and pronounced it not just "good," as He did when He brought Adam into being, but "very good" after creating Eve. If we start with the premise that differences between men and women are very good, we can then see the benefits of their various characteristics and understand how men and women can be complementary in carrying out God's purposes.

The fact of biological difference[3] explains some of the behavioral dissimilarities between women and men, but it does not account for all diversity. Some differences get picked up from the culture that shaped us but are neither innate to the person nor unchangeable. Generally, women and men communicate in different ways[4] even though we find no significant sex variation in intelligence.[5]

While some evidence suggests that sex differences in cognitive abilities (verbal, visual-spatial, and math abilities) diminish over time, the jury is still out, and for a number of reasons. The evolving nature of research methods used to study sex differences prevents us from concluding whether there are fewer differences between the sexes or if the ones previously observed were simply a function of biases embedded in those earlier tests. However, the differences in verbal abilities seem to advantage women, with men being stronger in only the area of verbal analogies. And the differences in visual-spatial abilities seem to favor men in four of the five types of abilities, but there is no sex difference in spatial visualization.

With regard to mathematical or quantitative abilities, elementary school age girls show superiority in computation while boys show advantages in problem solving. Yet as they mature into adolescence we see sex differences favoring males. Interestingly, there are no sex differences in the understanding of math concepts. We must, however, reiterate the paucity of conclusive studies suggesting that the differences in cognitive abilities diminish over time.[6] And the demonstration of cognitive abilities is not free of the effects of environmental factors. Thankfully, "we can all improve in our thinking with appropriate instruction."[7]

How Do They Lead? Or More Precisely, How *Should* They Lead?

Women lead in ways reflective of their environment, similar to the manner in which men do. Leadership is a function of both biology and culture. *How a culture relates to women and to men will prescribe and define the leadership styles and behaviors of both genders in that given culture.* Although boys and girls get socialized to lead in certain ways, the trend is toward a closing of the gap as parents seek to develop the leadership skills of girls and allow them to choose careers aligned with their particular talents and personalities. So maybe *how* women and men lead are not the best expressions of leadership.

Why do I say this? First, we are born in sin and shaped by sin, so our characters are defective, and God calls us to a restoration of the image of God.[8] Additionally, our culture is gendered, and gender-stereotyping activities have influenced parenting styles. We give girls dolls and encourage them to play "little mommy," while we hand boys toy soldiers and tell them to play "conqueror." Such stereotypical parenting and schooling activities are more likely than not to produce women who think their only role in life is to mother and men who believe they must compete and be aggressive. But such biased[9] and limited development of children deprives us of the Deborahs and the Lydias, whose lives God purposefully recorded in Scripture. Those women used their spiritual gifts to minister to God's people both before and after the appearance of our Savior, Jesus Christ. Let me illustrate with three noteworthy women leaders.

The prophet Deborah (Judges 4 and 5) was a wife, a prophet, and a judge. God called her to a leadership role that would deliver Israel from the Canaanites and their military leaders. And she courageously and unapologetically exercised leadership in a largely male military and political world.

The next noteworthy leader is Lydia (Acts 16). Recently I was on a tour of the seven churches, and while in Thyatira the tour guide, a leading archaeologist from Kusadasi, Turkey, referred to "the first European convert to Christianity." To my amazement, he identified her as Lydia, the seller of luxury linens favored by the wealthy. Because of the limitations of my Western orientation, I had not acknowledged her geographic region in that way. Lydia not only was a successful European businesswoman who became a Christian, but also was the head of her own household. Other people (possibly family members, servants, and slaves) were dependent upon her. And she not only provided for their economic support, but became, after discovering a message more precious than gold, the apostle to her household.

The Ellen G. White Estate records the following about one of the founders of the Seventh-day Adventist Church: "A woman of remarkable spiritual gifts." "She wrote more than 5,000 periodical articles and 40 books." "The most translated woman writer in the entire history of literature, and the most translated American author of either gender." "Seventh-day Adventists believe that Mrs. White was more than a gifted writer; they believe she was appointed by God as a special messenger to draw the world's attention to the Holy Scriptures and help prepare people for Christ's second advent."[10]

She led the early Seventh-day Adventist believers at a time before women could trace their empowerment to the outcomes of such social change as the women's suffrage movement in the United States.[11] Ellen White wrote, "Those who have the spiritual oversight of the church should devise ways and means by which an opportunity may be given to every member of the church to act some part in God's work. . . . The work of God in this earth can never be finished until the men *and women* comprising our church membership rally to the work, and unite their efforts with those of ministers and church officers."[12] As did Deborah, Ellen G. White called Christians to live lives of unflinching courage[13] and moral integrity.[14] And she modeled what she taught.

Men and women lead differently because of two factors: nature and nurture. Even when allowed to express who they are without the constrictions of social conventions, we may still see diversity in the ways men and women approach leadership, but the results of both remain the same. A woman who has been nurtured to be caring will lead with caring behaviors, an other-centeredness contrasting with the competitive and less risk-averse nature of most men. Yet studies of criminality show that women are as capable as men to be violent, murderous villains. What is the difference? Nurture and culture are powerful forces that shape behavior, whether in the direction of care for others or concern for self-interest. So while women are generally oriented to be nurturing, the environment in which they are raised may be typically slanted toward raising girls to be caregivers and nurturers while boys receive more latitude. As Christians we are to submit to God both our nature and how we have been nurtured. The Christian life is a choice to invite Him to restore the divine image within us.

Spiritual leadership entails deliberate choices to think and act in ways aligned with our aptitude, talents, and gifts. God does not say to men, Because you are a father you cannot also be a businessperson. Likewise, He does not tell a woman that because you are a mother you cannot also be a businessperson. Proverbs 31 says that a woman, like a man, has multiple roles and that she must develop herself to perform each chosen one to the best of her ability. Scripture also declares to *both* men and women that their primary role is that of parenting.[15] As with Deborah, Lydia, and Ellen G. White, women are called into a relationship with Jesus that mandates the sharing of their faith. And that is leadership.

When a Woman Is Called to Leadership in God's Cause, What Specific Qualities Does She Bring and What Challenges Will She Face?

Women engaged in spiritual leadership should recall the divine pronouncement after God made woman and praised the completeness of His creation. The Lord made it clear that Adam only partially reproduced His image. If we study only Adam and overlook the qualities God embedded in Eve, then we will not accurately perceive His reflected image in humanity. And women who respond to gender bias by imitating the leadership of men deny the blessing that God created Eve to deliver to His people. The image of God is conveyed in the mutuality and complementarity that the Lord fashioned Adam and Eve to demonstrate to the rest of creation. We see glimpses of that image of mutuality and other centeredness in the lives of godly women leaders both in Scripture and within the Christian church.

When God called Deborah, Lydia, and Ellen G. White to ministry, He did not shield them from the culture in which they served. We live (and they lived) within the constraints of culture. That is the reality of every society, whether we speak of culture at the national, geographic, or affinity group level. Ellen White demonstrated two qualities that women in positions of spiritual leadership will need: courage and humility. Leaders need courage to follow God's directions. And they must have humility to remain submissive to His will. It requires courage to withstand the biases and prejudices of both men and women toward women in leadership roles. And one must have humility because success in leadership can be its greatest danger!

Women leaders called to minister to others must obey God's call and fulfill that divine summons in ways that honor Him and support His work. If they do not respond to that divine call, they will not find rest in their souls. And when carrying out their duties they must maintain the humility demanded of all spiritual leaders. Miriam became puffed up and along with Aaron challenged Moses' unique call to lead the people of Israel.[16] As a result, she suffered God's punishment of leprosy. The call is not to a position but to minister on God's behalf. Again, we must return to the imperatives of the commission. Matthew's record of Jesus' words (Matt. 28:18-20) states that after we come to Jesus we must then "go," "baptize," and "teach" obedience to God's commands.

As I write the final words of the chapter, I pray that we can move beyond the current foment concerning women's ordination so that women leaders can fulfill their calling in a way that fully honors God and supports His worldwide work.

---

[1] In *Raise a Leader (God's Way)* (Hagerstown, Md.: Review and Herald Pub. Assn., 2012) I define leadership as an influence-building and empowering process.

[2] See 1 Corinthians 13 for a full development of the other-centeredness that God enumerated in Exodus 20, Matthew 5, and Luke 6.

[3] For a full treatment of the female brain and the cast of characters that make up the hormonal system and the relationship between hormones and control of brain functions, see Louann Brizendine, *The Female Brain* (New York: Morgan Road Books, 2006).

[4] See William B. Gudykunst, *Bridging Differences: Effective Intergroup Communication,* 3rd ed. (Thousand Oaks, Calif.: Sage Publications, 1998), pp. 88-90, for a discussion of gender communication differences. A more elaborate treatment of the topic appears in Deborah Tannen's best seller, *You Just Don't Understand: Women and Men in Conversation* (New York: Ballantine Books, 1990).

[5] University College London psychological researcher Adrian Furnham (2008) analyzed 30 studies and concluded that men are not smarter than women. They were found to be fairly equal overall in terms of IQ. But men think they are more intelligent than women, and it seems women underestimate their own intelligence and that of women in general. For the full interview with Joan Raymond, see "He's Not as Smart as He Thinks," *Newsweek,* Jan. 22, 2008.

[6] For an extensive treatment, see Diane F. Halpern, *Sex Differences in Cognitive Abilities,* 4th ed. (New York: Psychology Press, 2012).

[7] Jamie Hale's interview of Diane Halpern was accessed July 29, 2012, http://psych central.com/blog/archives/2011/04/24/analyzing-the-thinking-process-interview-with-diane-halpern/.

[8] Scripture refers to humanity's sinful nature, with notable mentions in Psalm 51:5 and Ephesians 2:3. Job 14:4 and 15:14 reflect on that nature and suggest that transformation must therefore come from outside, which we read about in John 3:16.

[9] For a scholarly development of the glass ceiling, refer to: Prudence L. Pollard, *"A Critical Analysis of the Glass Ceiling Phenomenon"* (Sloan Family and Work Encyclopedia, Carroll School of Management, Boston College, 2005).

[10] Retrieved from www.whiteestate.org/about/egwbio.asp, July 28, 2012.

[11] See the Nineteenth Amendment to the United States Constitution, which prohibits any United States citizen from being denied the right to vote based on sex.

[12] E. G. White, *Gospel Workers,* pp. 351, 352. (Italics supplied.)

[13] E. G. White, *The Acts of the Apostles,* p. 165.

[14] E. G. White, *Education,* p. 57.

[15] "Teach [the things your eyes have seen] to your children and your grandchildren" (Deut. 4:9, NKJV). "These words which I command you today shall be in your heart. You shall teach them diligently to your children" (Deut. 6:6-9, NKJV).

[16] See Numbers 12 for the biblical record of Aaron and Miriam's sin in wanting equal treatment for all the prophets (and themselves in particular) rather than what God ordained in setting Moses apart from the other prophets.

Chapter 7

THE PURPOSEFUL LEADER

Dan Jackson

PRESIDENT, NORTH AMERICAN DIVISION OF SEVENTH-DAY ADVENTISTS

S uccessful Christian leaders can look back to the time when they first saw the dream—the God-given vision that compelled them to do what they do and to go where they have gone. As a result, they have arrived at their destination because they have followed God-inspired, clearly laid out purposes. They have spent time immersing themselves in divine things, and then they have moved forward with clarity.

Success does not materialize in a vacuum. We have to determine that to succeed as a Christian leader we must be committed primarily to bringing glory to God—to be used in the advancement of His kingdom.

People who think that success "just happens" are dreamers who remind me of the words I once saw emblazoned on a multidirectional, double-brimmed hat. It simply read "These are my people, I must follow them. Which way did they go?" Success and purpose are highly related.

Many years ago now, in the early years of my ministry, I learned a leadership lesson that I have never forgotten. The principles gleaned from that experience have enabled me to walk through multiple circumstances with a level of assurance that has been a blessing.

We all stood there side by side watching the earthmoving machine work. Its powerful engine groaned as the huge blade cut into the ground. Soon it had excavated a hole big enough to suit our need. We had decided to build a church, and this was the beginning—or was it?

Conference leaders had asked our family to move to this place, and we had accepted the call, primarily because we wanted our children to receive a quality Adventist Christian education in the academy located there. My previous congregation had just voted not to have a school, and so the decision, though emotionally difficult, was fairly easy from a practical perspective. However, we did not envision what lay ahead in our newly adopted congregation. As a matter of fact, the new relationship didn't start on a real bright note when on the first Sabbath someone introduced me in the following way: "Well, our pastor is gone, and now we have Pastor Jackson." It just didn't ring with that note of optimism and enthusiasm that one might expect.

You see, prior to accepting the call I was totally unaware of what had been happening in the life of that congregation. Though they had taken no formal action, most of the members had decided that their particular church had no future. Many of them had already decided what new congregation to join when our church closed down. They had lost their beloved pastor and, with him, their dreams of a new edifice. They were suffering from a significant bout of congregational depression. After all, the area had several other congregations, and the transition would be smooth.

Shortly after assuming my responsibilities, I came to understand their condition and their plans. My heart stirred by their pain, I determined that I would do everything I could to help them. However, I did not want to be the pastor of a congregation that didn't want to be a congregation. I called a business meeting to clarify the situation.

On the evening of that meeting I took what I call a "sanctified gamble" when I asked the members to decide "that very night" as to whether or not they would remain a congregation. I believe that the Lord nudged me to do it, because they decided to stay together and to carry on.

In the days and weeks following that meeting I discovered that their expectations of a future church building significantly outstripped their potential as a group. On top of that, it seemed to me that they had lost sight of their original mission objectives. Consequently, I went about visiting the members in an attempt to understand their perspectives of how things had unfolded as they had. They responded positively and constructively, and out of all of this another vision emerged. We entered another phase of congregational life called *building!*

We bonded as a group, adjusted our vision, outlined our mission within the community at large, and decided to construct a much-scaled-down church. Most important, we would minister to our world.

And now we stood there on the edge of that hole watching it grow larger and larger. We were all so happy. However, as that Caterpillar tractor droned on that morning, I moved a few yards away from the majority of the members. Then I heard it! It was music to my ears. I have often said that it was the greatest compliment ever paid to me as a leader. It went like this: "Look what we have done. Praise God!" Not only had they bought into a new dream—they had taken possession of it. While I praised God for that moment, I also praised Him for the insight into the minds of my new members.

I tell this story not to celebrate compliments or accomplishments but rather to look at some of the basic principles of purposeful Christian leadership. If properly understood and implemented, such concepts can enable new leaders to chart a course that will allow them to navigate the challenging waters of administration today.

Principle 1: Build an Atmosphere of Confidence.

Commonly called buy-in, it lies at the root of everything leaders do. The first significant question they must ask is How do I create an atmosphere whereby those I lead will be open to consider and then accept my proposals? An administrator with purpose will recognize that as important as their goals might be, they must first prepare the ground for dialogue. If you don't do such groundwork through connecting with people, the obstacles you will face may become overwhelming.

Jesus provides us with a wonderful example of a winning leadership style. His life and mission were very purposeful, and yet even He who originated creativity itself still worked carefully with people. He demonstrated by the way He operated that in order to lead people He would first need to create the right atmosphere. Because He was well aware of the human condition and the circumstances that shaped the lives of those He worked with on a daily basis, Jesus knew that the only way to be able to introduce them to the great truths He had to offer was by winning their confidence. He accomplished that by demonstrating a genuine interest in them.

The writings of John clearly help us to see His impact. "Jesus went through all the towns and villages, teaching in their synagogues, proclaiming the good news of the kingdom and healing every disease and sickness. When He saw the crowds, he had compassion on them, because they were harassed and helpless, like sheep without a shepherd" (Matt. 9:35, 36, NIV). Why did men and women accept Jesus' authority and subsequently His plans and ideas? Their positive response came as a result of understanding His good will for them. They could see His unquestionable interest in them and therefore opened their minds to His teaching.

Ellen While further elaborates on this idea when she counseled the leaders of both her day and ours by saying that: "Christ's method alone will give true success in reaching the people. The Savior mingled with men as one who desired their good. He showed His sympathy for them, ministered to their needs, and won their confidence. Then He bade them, 'Follow Me.'"[1]

Genuine authority in leadership doesn't come with title or position but when we so identify with the needs and aspirations of others that they can see and feel our passion. People recognize transparency, and as a result they respond with openness. Subsequently, they are willing to follow and implement our ideas.

Principle 2: Know Yourself.

A second significant principle that will enable the purposeful Christian leader to succeed is that of self-knowledge. William Shakespeare wrote the following words of counsel: "This above all: To thine own self be true, and it must follow, as the night the day, thou canst not then be false to any man."[2] Nothing is more dangerous to leadership than the individual who is not self-aware. I am not speaking of arrogant self-confidence or of egotistical self-assurance. Rather, I am simply referring to our acknowledgment of our strengths, weaknesses, and susceptibilities. As leaders we not only must be fully aware of who we are personally but also must have a knowledge of to whom we belong.

In his letter to the believers in Rome the apostle Paul wrote: "The Spirit himself testifies with our spirit that we are God's children. Now if we are children, then we are heirs—heirs of God and co-heirs with Christ" (Rom. 8:16, 17, NIV). As purposeful leaders we need to be in touch with our own feelings, with our own humanity. We must also constantly keep in mind that we are children of God and heirs of the promises He has made. Ultimately, our authority to lead comes out of our connection to the Lord and not our own abilities.

Jesus had self-awareness. Throughout His life He often found Himself challenged by others on the question of His origins. While His lifestyle and actions demonstrated His intense connection with His Father, He also made straightforward statements that left no doubt in minds and hearts that He knew He was the Messiah, the Son of the living God.

A clear illustration appears in His encounter with the woman at the well. Here within the context of winning her confidence Jesus demonstrated that He was very clearly aware of who He was. After the full discussion of men and mountains and faith the woman made one last attempt to outsmart our Lord. " 'I know that Messiah' (called Christ) 'is coming. When he comes, he will explain everything to us.' Then Jesus declared, 'I, the one speaking to you—I am he' " (John 4:25, 26, NIV). At that point the woman ran to share the good news.

As leaders possessed with a mission we need to clearly understand ourselves and share with others that we, along with them, are children of God and that He has done things for us that He will also do for them. When we connect in this way—and with genuine authenticity—men and women become open to listening to our ideas and following our dreams with us.

However, as significant as demonstrating our self-awareness and authenticity are to effective Christian leadership, such elements are not an end in themselves. A leader with a mission must demonstrate that they know not only where they come from but also where they are going.

Principle 3: Be a Learner and Be Flexible.

Our self-knowledge should also bring the realization that we cannot lead without understanding the people we lead. Furthermore, after researching and coming to understand the group we are responsible for, as Christian leaders we must be flexible, able to adjust to the realities around us. An old proverb put it well: "He who knows not, and knows not that he knows not, is a fool; avoid him. He who knows not, and knows that he knows not, is a wise man; teach him." From a biblical perspective the path to wisdom lies in our recognition of our limitations. Paul makes this observation in a rather strong way when he says, "If any of you think you are wise by the standards of this age, you should become 'fools' so that you may become wise" (1 Cor. 3:18, NIV).

Many years ago I had the privilege of attending an Andrews University Field School of Evangelism conducted by Don Jacobsen in Shrewsbury, Wales. It was a blessed and educative experience. However, the greatest lesson I gleaned from it centered on being flexible. He commenced the meetings in a traditional manner, based upon his extensive evangelistic experience. However, when he saw that the method was not working, he adjusted. He was not so focused on his own approach to evangelism that he could not flex.

The fact that you have become a leader is not synonymous with being gifted with all of the world's knowledge. Get to know the people you are leading and adjust to the new realities you may find, as long as those shifts do not involve spiritual compromise.

Principle 4: Keep the Main Thing the Main Thing.

How do successful leaders keep the big picture in mind and communicate it to those they are leading?

Sometime ago author David Campbell wrote a book entitled *If You Don't Know Where You're Going, You'll Probably End Up Somewhere Else.* The idea that jumps out at us as we read this title is that if we are not clear about our purpose and direction, competing ideas and distractions can take us off course. The result is that our plans may become convoluted. Intentionality is indispensable here.

Jesus' ministry was directed. He had a big-picture plan and consistently stayed on course. While He lived in "the shadow of the cross," He moved with purpose as He pursued His goals. To the Pharisees who challenged His authenticity He responded: "Even if I testify on my own behalf, my testimony is valid, for I know where I came from and where I am going" (John 8:14, NIV). The book of Hebrews urges the Hebrew Christians to follow the pattern that Jesus had laid out. It tells them and us to "run with perseverance the race marked out for us, fixing our eyes on Jesus, the pioneer and perfecter of faith. For the joy set before him he endured the cross, scorning its shame, and sat down at the right hand of the throne of God" (Heb. 12:1, 2, NIV).

Years ago when the Adventist Health System was not as strong as it is today, a leader by the name of Mardian Blair developed a long-term vision of excellence. His plan included the recruitment of the best and brightest minds from our Seventh-day Adventist colleges and universities. He dreamed of taking these young minds and molding them into top-flight administrators, directors, and leaders. While the idea at the time must have seemed tedious, he stuck with his plan. One does not have to make long arguments in terms of his eventual success. Observation tells the story. Because he pursued his vision, the system today is one of the finest anywhere.

Our purposes as leaders must be God-inspired, bold enough to capture the imagination of those who follow, and yet simple enough for anyone to understand. As we lay our plans before God, He will show us whether we are to proceed or to go back to the drawing board. One thing is certain: as we work for the advancement of His cause, God has promised to stand at our side. Jeremiah reminds of this fact in that great statement of divine assurance " 'For I know the plans I have for you,' declares the Lord, 'plans to prosper you and not to harm you, plans to give you hope and a future' " (Jer. 29:11, NIV). Jesus walks among the candlesticks of our need and blesses our efforts (see Rev. 1:12-19).

---

[1] E. G. White, *The Ministry of Healing,* p. 143.
[2] *Hamlet,* Act I, scene 3, lines 78-80.

Chapter 8

THE LEADER'S CHARACTER

Ella Smith Simmons

VICE PRESIDENT, GENERAL CONFERENCE OF SEVENTH-DAY ADVENTISTS

When I looked up the word *character* in one Internet reference source, the first definition it provided referred to and presented a large example of the beautiful calligraphy characters of Chinese and Japanese writing. Interestingly, many Chinese and Japanese young people are forgetting the calligraphy of their traditional languages. For example, a poll conducted by *China Youth Daily* (April 2010) "found that 83 percent of over 2,000 respondents admitted to having difficulty remembering how to write certain characters." Some in the media are calling the phenomenon "character amnesia."

Many attribute this phenomenon to an increasing dependence on computers and smartphones. Although users learned the traditional characters in childhood and recognize the characters when they see them, they no longer can reproduce them from memory. Technology has made it easy for them to type in the pinyin (a romanized spelling of Chinese words) and instantly receive back the character, resulting in a neglect of traditional handwriting. Many argue that need for such writing is obsolete now and that traditional calligraphy is no longer necessary.[1]

Some people, young and old, in all parts of the world, have character amnesia of a different type. "When faced with a dilemma, they seem to 'forget' the right thing to do and instead choose the easy way out."[2]

The world cannot afford character amnesia in life situations, particularly in leadership, for as Blackaby and Blackaby (2001) observe, "it is character that enables a person to lead."[3] Such character is who we are—not a skill that we can set aside or forget. Thomas Paine once observed that "character is much better kept than recovered." He is also known to have distinguished between character and reputation, declaring that "reputation is what men and women think of us; character is what God and angels know of us."[4]

Defining Elements of Character

Character is one of those taken-for-granted notions of everyday life, and yet is an ethereal perception fully discerned only by God. Often in the fallibility of human frailty we confuse personality for character. Typically, personality is more closely associated with temperament, disposition, and nature. Character for our purpose here is what distinguishes individuals on the basis of deeper traits and values.

Philosophers and poets alike have held that character is the cumulative effect of habits of thought and behavior practiced over time. A composite of all the qualities and features that make a person fundamentally unique from others, it pertains to moral strength.

Importance of Character for Leadership

Given its significance in human identity and its concomitant power for directing human behavior, it is reasonable to deduce that character is the primary determining factor in leadership. Thus character is the most essential element, for it encompasses all the other qualities that comprise the leadership package. It is the grand combination of integrity, kindness, courtesy, respectfulness, tenderness, sympathy, loyalty, humility, confidence, responsibility, self-discipline, teachable spirit, and trust, to name several.

So then one might ask What does "good" character look like in action, and how does it manifest itself in the everyday life of a leader? Both the research and self-help literature support the significance of character. Secular and religious publications alike regard character as essential to leadership.[5]

For example, a popular institute for character education for youth describes its program as one based on "six ethical values that everyone can agree on—values that are not political, religious, or culturally biased." They state their six pillars of character and related behavior in refreshingly clear and simple terms:

Trustworthiness.
Be honest. Don't deceive, cheat, or steal. Be reliable—do what you say

you'll do. Have the courage to do the right thing. Build a good reputation. Be loyal.

Respect.

Treat others with respect and follow the golden rule. Be tolerant and accepting of differences. Use good manners, not bad language. Be considerate of the feelings of others. Don't threaten or hurt anyone. Deal peacefully with anger, insults, and disagreements.

Responsibility.

Do what you are supposed to do. Plan ahead. Persevere: keep on trying! Always do your best. Use self-control. Be self-disciplined. Think before you act—consider the consequences. Be accountable for your words, actions, and attitudes. Set a good example for others.

Fairness.

Play by the rules. Share. Be open-minded and listen to others. Don't take advantage of others. Don't blame others carelessly. Treat all people fairly.

Caring.

Be kind. Be compassionate and show that you care. Express gratitude. Forgive others. Help people in need.

Citizenship.

Do your share to make your [organization] and community better. Cooperate. Get involved in community affairs. Stay informed; vote. Be a good neighbor. Obey laws and rules. Respect authority. Protect the environment. Volunteer.[6]

Jim Collins, in his best seller on organizational strength, *Good to Great* (2001), offers a rejection of "the old adage that people [in the organization] are your most important asset." He says, "In a good-to-great transformation, people are not your most important asset. The *right* people are."[7]

Reflecting on the practices of a successful organization, Collins comments that "in determining 'the right people,' the good-to-great companies placed greater weight on character attributes than on specific educational background, practical skills, specialized knowledge, or work experience."[8]

In distinguishing between managers and leaders, Warren Bennis observes, "managers are people who do things right, while leaders are people who do the right thing." On organizational excellence Bennis notes that "excellence starts with leaders of good and strong character who engage in the entire process of leadership. And the first process is being a person of honorable character."[9]

From his study Bennis identified six personal qualities for successful leadership. All are elements of character. They include:

Integrity.

Alignment of words and actions with inner values; sticking to such values even when an alternative path may be easier or more advantageous. A leader with integrity can be trusted and will be admired for adhering to strong values. They also act as a powerful model for people to copy, thus building an entire organization with strong and effective cultural values.

Dedication.

Spending whatever time and energy a task requires to get the job done, rather than giving it whatever time you have available. The work of most leadership positions is not something to do "if time allows." It means giving your whole self to the task, dedicating yourself to success and to leading others with you.

Magnanimity.

Giving credit where it is due; being gracious in defeat and permitting others to retain their dignity even if they lose. In leadership such magnanimity includes crediting other people with success and accepting personal responsibility for failure.

Humility.

The opposite of arrogance and narcissism; recognizing that you are not inherently superior to others and consequently that they are not inferior to you. It does not mean diminishing yourself, nor does it mean exalting yourself. Humble leaders do not debase themselves, neither falsely nor because of low self-esteem. They simply recognize all people as equal in value and know that their position does not make them a god.

Openness.

Being able to listen to ideas outside one's current mental models and suspending judgment until after one has heard someone else's ideas. An open leader listens to their people without trying to shut them down early, which at least demonstrates care and builds trust. Also, openness treats other ideas as potentially better than one's own. In the uncertain world of new territory, being able to consider alternatives is an important skill.

Creativity.

The ability to think differently, to get outside the box and take a new and different viewpoint on things. For a leader to be able to see a new future toward which they will lead their followers, creativity provides the ability to think differently and see things that others have not yet recognized, thus providing further reason for others to follow.[10]

Renee Davies has analyzed the literature on character from a Christian perspective on leadership. She cites research by Bennis that outlines five common competencies that leaders share: technical ability, interpersonal skills, conceptual skills, judgment, and character (1999). She points out that "of the five competencies, Bennis claims that character is the vital element that determines a leader's effectiveness, adding that 'leaders rarely fail because of technical incompetence' but more so for lack of character."[11]

Leadership scandals of the past few decades have raised public consciousness and concerns about the leaders in business, government, nonprofit agencies, and religious institutions. In this context the Barna Research Group initiated a study that examined the character of church leaders. Their study examined four aspects of leadership: the sense of calling from God to leadership, the nature of character, the strength of competencies, and the aptitude for leadership. In the process their research identified the character traits that are generally strongest among church leaders and those that are most likely to be the weak links.

The Barna Group reported that the strongest attributes associated with those in church leadership involved having a conscience sensitive to sin, strong morality, godly demeanor, humility, values, faith maturity, and trustworthiness. They found that "character is not like competencies, for which it is acceptable to ignore your weaknesses and run with your strengths. Weakness of character will eventually undermine your strengths, no matter how strong they are."[12]

Cindy Tutsch in her study of the writings of Ellen White on leadership articulated the need of leaders for character development through a series of 10 observations:

1. The leader's integrity and character are predicated on time with God.
2. For the leader, both blessings and challenges call for dependence on God.
3. The leader's care for the poor develops character.
4. High administrative leadership position and extreme pressure mandate dependence on God.
5. The leader's obedience and trust in God, not position, make character.
6. God's leadership transcends humanity's.
7. The leader makes wisdom a higher priority than wealth, power, or fame.
8. The leader's character development is more essential than church business.
9. For the leader, praise and high profile can corrupt.
10. The leader's age, power, and position don't guarantee holiness of character.[13]

Scriptural Portrayal of Character

What does the Bible have to say about character? It speaks of good or desirable character as a good name. Scripture distinguishes between the character of the saints and that of the wicked.

It describes the saints (that is, a desirable character) as being attentive to Christ's voice (John 10:3, 4); blameless and harmless (Phil. 2:15). Followers of Christ—those of good character (John 10:4, 27)—are bold (Prov. 28:1); contrite (Isa. 57:15; 66:2); devout (Acts 8:2; 22:12); and faithful (Rev. 17:14). Furthermore, Scripture describes them as guileless (John 1:47); holy (Deut. 7:6; 14:2; Col. 3:12); just (Gen. 6:9; Hab. 2:4; Luke 2:25); and humble (Ps. 34:2; 1 Peter 5:5). Led by the Spirit (Rom. 8:14), they are liberal (Isa. 32:8; 2 Cor. 9:13) and loathe their fallen nature (Eze. 20:43).

The saints are loving (Col. 1:4; 1 Thess. 4:9); lowly (Prov. 16:19); meek (Isa. 29:19; Matt. 5:5); and merciful (Ps. 37:26; Matt. 5:7). In addition, they are obedient (Rom. 16:19; 1 Peter 1:14); poor in spirit (Matt. 5:3); prudent (Prov. 16:21); pure in heart (Matt. 5:8; 1 John 3:3); righteous (Isa. 60:21; Luke 1:6); sincere (2 Cor. 1:12; 2:17); and steadfast (Acts 2:42; Col. 2:5). God's people are true (2 Cor. 6:8); undefiled (Ps. 119:1); upright (1 Kings 3:6; Ps. 15:2); watchful (Luke 12:37); and zealous for good works (Titus 2:14).

In stark contrast the Bible describes the character of the wicked as abominable (Rom. 1:28-31; Rev. 21:8) and blasphemous (Luke 22:65; Rev. 16:9). They are said to be blinded (2 Cor. 4:4; Eph. 4:18); boastful (Ps. 10:3; 49:6); conspiratorial (Neh. 4:8; 6:2; Ps. 38:12); corrupt (Matt. 7:17; Eph. 4:22); covetous (Micah 2:2; Rom. 1:29); deceitful (Ps. 5:6; Rom. 3:13); delighting in the iniquity of others (Prov. 2:14; Rom. 1:32); and despising the saints (Neh. 2:19; 4:2; 2 Tim. 3:3, 4). Scripture depicts them as destructive (Isa. 59:7); disobedient (Neh. 9:26; Titus 3:3; 1 Peter 2:7); enticing others to evil (Prov. 1:10-14; 2 Tim. 3:6); envious (Neh. 2:10; Titus 3:3); evildoers (Jer. 13:23; Micah 7:3); fearful (Prov. 28:1; Rev. 21:8); fierce (Prov. 16:29; 2 Tim. 3:3); and foolish (Deut. 32:6; Ps. 5:5).

The Word says that they are fraudulent (Ps. 37:21; Micah 6:11); perverse (Deut. 32:5; see also Prov. 21:8, NKJV); hard-hearted (Eze. 3:7); hating the light (Job 24:13; John 3:20); headstrong (2 Tim. 3:4); and hypocritical (Isa. 29:13; 2 Tim. 3:5). They are impudent (Eze. 2:4) and without self-control (2 Tim. 3:3). Scripture terms them infidels (Ps. 10:4; 14:1); loathsome (Prov. 13:5); untruthful (Ps. 58:3; 62:4; Isa. 59:4); mischievous (Prov. 24:8; Micah 7:3); murderous (Ps. 10:8; 94:6; Rom. 1:29); and persecuting (Ps. 69:26; 109:16).

Furthermore, God's Word sees them as proud (Ps. 59:12; Obadiah 3; 2 Tim. 3:2); rebellious (Isa. 1:2; 30:9); reprobate (2 Cor. 13:5; 2 Tim. 3:8; Titus 1:16); selfish (2 Tim. 3:2); sensual (Phil. 3:19; Jude 19); stiff-hearted (Eze. 2:4); stiff-necked (Ex. 33:5; Acts 7:51); unjust (Prov. 11:7); unmerciful (Rom. 1:31); unholy (2 Tim. 3:2); unprofitable (Matt. 25:30; Rom. 3:12); unruly (Titus 1:10); unthankful (Luke 6:35; 2 Tim. 3:2); corrupt (see Acts 2:40, NIV); and unwise (Deut. 32:6).

Formation of Character

Character is the aim of child rearing and the quest of corporate recruitment. It is the goal of self-development and the end of salvific transformation. Ellen G. White observed that character development is the work of a lifetime.[14] Yet character is essential for successful life at all stages.

Although character development spans the life, we acquire it step by step. "The spiritual leader's personal growth is the accumulation of God's activity in his or her life."[15] Sow a thought, reap an act; sow an act, reap a habit; sow a habit, reap a character; sow a character, reap a destiny (traditional saying, source unknown). As a person "thinketh in his heart, so is he" (Prov. 23:7). Many thoughts make up the unwritten history of a single day, and they have much to do with the formation of character. They can quicken the spiritual pulse and increase the power for doing good. The longest journey is performed by taking one step at a time. A succession of steps brings us to the end of the road. Thus it is with character. A well-balanced character is formed by single acts well performed.[16]

"In every generation . . . the true foundation for character building has been the same—the principles contained in the word of God. The only safe and sure rule is to do what God says."[17] The knowledge of God, as Christ revealed, "is the knowledge that works transformation of character."[18]

"The formation of a right character is . . . the outgrowth of prayerful meditation united with a grand purpose. The excellence of character that you possess must be the result of your own effort. Friends may encourage you, but they cannot do the work for you. Wishing, sighing, dreaming, will never make you great or good. You must climb."[19] "The conversation we have by the fireside, the books we read, the business we transact, are all agents in forming our characters, and day by day decide our eternal destiny."[20]

"The heavenly intelligences will work with the human agent who seeks with determined faith that perfection of character which will reach out to perfection in action."[21] "He who would build up a strong, symmetrical character, he who would be a well-balanced Christian, must give all and do all for Christ; for the Redeemer will not accept divided service. Daily he must learn the meaning of self-surrender. He must study the word of God, learning its meaning and obeying its precepts. Thus he may reach the standard of Christian excellence. Day by day God works with him, perfecting the character that is to stand in the time of final test."[22]

Summary

A few years back *U.S. News and World Report* highlighted the nation's top leaders and in the same article decried leadership as being in a sad state (Oct. 31, 2005). One could observe the same for the entire world. Ellen White declared a century ago that "the greatest want of the world is the want of men—men who will not be bought or sold, men who in their inmost souls are true and honest, men who do not fear to call sin by its right name, men whose conscience is as true to duty as the needle to the pole, men who will stand for the right though the heavens fall."[23]

"But such a character is not the result of accident; it is not due to special favors or endowments of Providence. A noble character is the result of self-discipline, of the subjection of the lower to the higher nature—the surrender of self for the service of love to God and man."[24]

"Mental ability and genius are not character, for these are often possessed by those who have the very opposite of a good character. Reputation is not character. True character is a quality of the soul, revealing itself in the conduct."[25]

"A good character is a capital of more value than gold or silver. It is unaffected by panics or failures, and in that day when earthly possessions shall be swept away, it will bring rich returns. Integrity, firmness, and perseverance are qualities that all should seek earnestly to cultivate; for they clothe the possessor with a power which is irresistible—a power which makes him strong to do good, strong to resist evil, strong to bear adversity."[26]

"Those whose souls are not united to the eternal Rock will be swept away by the worldly current. We can stand firm only as our life is hid with Christ in God."[27] There can be no character amnesia. "We are not to elevate our standard just a little above the world's standard, but we are to make the distinction decidedly apparent. . . . [Many teachers or leaders] do not keep the divine plan ever in view, but are fixing their eyes upon worldly models."[28]

Christian leaders should look to Peter's ladder of eight rounds (2 Peter 1:5-7). Christ, who connects earth with heaven, is the ladder. The base is planted firmly on the earth in His humanity while the topmost round reaches to the throne of God in His divinity. Faith, virtue, knowledge, temperance, patience, godliness, brotherly kindness, and charity form the rounds of this ladder. All must manifest themselves in the Christian character.[29]

"None need fail of attaining, in his sphere, to perfection of Christian character. By the sacrifice of Christ, provision has been made for the believer to receive all things that pertain to life and godliness. God calls upon us to reach the standard of perfection and places before us the example of Christ's character. In His humanity, perfected by a life of constant resistance of evil, the Savior showed that through cooperation with Divinity, human beings may in this life attain to perfection of character. This is God's assurance to us that we, too, may obtain complete victory."[30]

---

[1] *Asia Society*, Aug. 27, 2010.

[2] Cindy Hess Kasper, "Character Amnesia," *Our Daily Bread Radio*, Sept. 13, 2011, hosted by Les Lamborn.

[3] Henry T. Blackaby and Richard Blackaby, *Spiritual Leadership* (Nashville: Broadman and Holman Pub., 2001), p. 112.

[4] In Martin H. Manser, comp., *The Westminster Collection of Christian Quotations* (Louisville, Ky.: Westminster John Knox Press, 2001).

[5] Warren Bennis and Robert Townsend, *Reinventing Leadership* (New York: HarperCollins, 2005); Jim Collins, "Level 5 Leadership," *Harvard Business Review*, January 2001; Cindy Tutsch, *Ellen White on Leadership* (Nampa, Idaho: Pacific Press Pub. Assn., 2008).

[6] Michael Josephson, *Making Ethical Decisions* (Josephson Institute Center for Youth Ethics, 2011).

[7] Jim Collins, *Good to Great* (New York: HarperCollins, 2001), p. 51.

[8] *Ibid.*

[9] "Character and Traits in Leadership," www.nwlink.com/~donclark/leader/leadchr.html.

[10] See Josephson.

[11] www.answersforme.org/article/252/find-answers/career/three-hidden-qualities-of-great-leaders.

[12] www.barna.org/barna-update/article/5-barna-update/113-new-study-identifies-the-strongest-and-weakest-character-traits-of-christian-leaders?q=generational+differences.

[13] Cindy Tutsch, *Ellen White on Leadership: Guidance for Those Who Influence Others* (Nampa, Idaho: Pacific Press Pub. Assn., 2008), pp. 35-38.

[14] See E. G. White, *Counsels to Parents, Teachers, and Students,* p. 61.

[15] Blackaby and Blackaby, p. 112.

[16] Ellen G. White, *Messages to Young People* (Nashville: Southern Pub. Assn., 1930), p. 144.

[17] E. G. White, *The Acts of the Apostles,* p. 475.

[18] *Ibid.*

[19] Ellen G. White, *My Life Today* (Washington, D.C.: Review and Herald Pub. Assn., 1952), p. 267.

[20] *Ibid.*

[21] E. G. White, *Christ's Object Lessons,* p. 332.

[22] E. G. White, *The Acts of the Apostles,* p. 483

[23] E. G. White, *Education*, p. 57.

[24] *Ibid.*

[25] E. G. White, *My Life Today,* p. 267.

[26] *Ibid.*

[27] E. G. White, *Testimonies,* vol. 6, p. 146.

[28] *Ibid.*, pp. 146, 147.

[29] See *ibid.*, p. 147; see also Clive Anderson, *Opening Up 2 Peter*, Opening Up the Bible (Leominster, U.K.: Day One Publications, 2007), pp. 26-30.

[30] E. G. White, *The Acts of the Apostles,* p. 531.

Chapter 9

THE LEADER'S VISION

Leslie Pollard

PRESIDENT, OAKWOOD UNIVERSITY

There can be no leadership without vision! Thousands of studies have attempted to identify the skills, attitudes, and behaviors that create leadership effectiveness. While they have not identified any single attribute or behavior as the "silver bullet" that makes us effective leaders, the ideas of vision and focus consistently appear in the major scientific studies of leadership. This chapter addresses the crucial role that vision plays. John Kotter, a famous organizational development consultant, wrote: "A vision helps to clarify the direction in which an organization needs to move."[1] Every day, leaders, in the midst of a flood tide of unrelenting responsibilities and demands, risk losing their vision. Consider the following illustration from church history:

A deeply discouraged blind man once listened to a sermon by the ancient cleric Anthony. The sermon focused on the trials that beset Christian believers—heartache, pain, and suffering. As the cleric continued preaching, the blind man became increasingly agitated. Finally he stood to his feet and blurted out, "Anthony, can anything be worse than losing your sight?" After pausing for a moment, the great preacher replied, "Yes, my friend—losing your vision!"

Leadership today is increasingly complex. Followers are different. The information revolution has altered the landscape of leadership. And the failures of leaders has contributed in some places to skepticism. Before I write about the matter of vision, however, I wish to share a few perspectives vital to understanding the role that leadership plays in the accomplishment of mission.

Perspectives Needed for Leadership Effectiveness

The first perspective that shapes our discussion on leadership and vision is the assumption that effective spiritual leadership is crucial to mission accomplishment. In every instance in which God's people rose to meet their challenges in exceptional ways, we find a passionate commitment of support for faith-based leadership. Whether the leader was Nehemiah, David, Elijah, Deborah, Ruth, or Esther, they preserved God's glory and elevated His mission, because they were willing to put God's mission ahead of personal considerations.

A second foundational principle for Christian leaders is that of God's vision as indicated in Scripture, not the leader's vision. A great temptation facing every leader in a missional organization will be to replace the divine vision for the growth of God's work with similar but substitute visions. There will always be many worthy visions—e.g., self-help rather than self-crucifixion, social gospel versus personal transformation, church-as-social-fraternity versus church-as-missional-enterprise—that compete for the heart, mind, and energy of the leader. But true kingdom advancement has consistently taken place when God's leaders have adhered to His vision versus any other.

A third perspective of mine is the assumption that putting God's vision into practice will change both leaders and followers. My personal experience with faith-based leadership across the past 35 years has reminded me that personal transformation lies in submission to God's way and will. His will for His work is the single imperative that must control everything we do. Jacob submitted to God's vision in Genesis 32, and his entire life changed, including his name (see verses 24-31). The Lord placed within Jacob (and us) the power needed to rise above circumstances and to affect the lives of others. Note the following story by David Schaal:

"As Christians we may be compared with a reservoir for producing electrical power, like one of those you see when you drive down the canyon. When we accept Christ, construction of our reservoir is complete. We now have the potential to be useful and to affect lives. But until the floodgates are opened and the cascading river waters pour through, no power is realized. So it is when we are baptized in the Holy Spirit. We open our lives to God and the Holy Spirit pours into us and through us. It is then we become most effective in God's service. As with the reservoir, this power-generating experience is not intended to be a one-time occurrence. It is to be an ongoing process. When our spiritual power runs low, we need to return to the Source and let the blessed Holy Spirit pour into us again, bringing fresh power."[2]

Vision—A Definition

Here is my personal definition of leadership vision: it is the leader's presentation (in speech and action) of tomorrow's realities today. The leader's vision communicates the desired future for the organization. Vision is the dream that orients present organizational action—the metaperspective from which a leader guides.

Authentic leaders are visionaries. Whether it is Bill Gates envisioning a computer on every desk; Martin Luther King, Jr., sharing with a wearied nation in 1963, "I have a dream"; John the revelator declaring, "I saw a new heaven and a new earth"; Michelangelo seeing angels in stone; Eleanor Roosevelt envisioning a world of equal opportunity for women and minorities; John F. Kennedy famously dreaming of putting a man on the moon; or Ellen G. White envisioning the Advent message, vision is what separates leaders from their generation. As streams of light, circling the entire world, every great stride into the future has resulted because someone, somewhere, had a vision of progress. Robert Kennedy, in his paraphrase of George Bernard Shaw, poignantly expressed the nature of vision: "Some people see things as they are, and ask *why?* I dream of things that never were, and ask *why not?*" Visionaries go and take us where no else has ever gone before.

Vision and Visionaries—Seven Characteristics

1. **Visionaries are not bound by local circumstances.** The visionary leader moves beyond the present circumstances to the future. Notice what Ellen G. White wrote: "Man can shape circumstances, but circumstances should not be allowed to shape the man. We should seize upon circumstances as instruments by which to work. We are to master them, but should not permit them to master us."[3] At a minimum, the visionary leader looks beyond the present to see future possibilities.

2. **Visionaries dream beyond local geography to create a tangible contribution of universal significance.** As an example, Ellen G. White saw the Adventist message streaming around the world.

She, like many other leaders of vision, elevated followers above local boundaries. People of vision may act locally, but they think globally.

3. **Vision is transformational.** It inspires both followers and leaders to reach higher, stretch further, run faster, and dig deeper. A major leadership theory describes transformational leaders as possessing at least two qualities—vision and personal interest in their followers. The greatest example that the world has ever known is Jesus Christ. He communicated to His followers His vision for a global mission during the three and a half years of His ministry. And because of His deep interest in them—one so great that He died for them—they saw something more than parochial Palestine. They actually believed that they could be global ambassadors of the message of Jesus Christ. The fact that we are members of the worldwide body of Jesus Christ is evidence that He transformed the original disciples into international ambassadors for the Christian faith.

4. **Vision orients our leadership compass amid distractions.** In rebuilding the wall at Jerusalem, Nehemiah faced many difficulties and detractors. But as we see in the book of Nehemiah, his vision for the restoration of God's city served as his compass that kept him on task. It also anchored his follower's commitments. When asked to step away from his mission to engage his critics, he declared in Nehemiah 6:3, "I am doing a great work and I cannot come down" (NASB). His workers did not get discouraged but continued in the face of opposition and criticism to rebuild the walls. That is the power of vision.

5. **Visionaries have the power to make the future present.** One of the most striking aspects of John the revelator was his ability to close the gap between the present and the future. His leadership power turned on his spiritual giftedness and God's vision of the superiority of the coming world over the present one. Later Ellen White's visions also brought the known present and the unknown future together. While visionaries cannot exhaustively describe the coming reality, they can pull us closer to God's desired future.

6. **Vision provides perseverance and missional energy.** In one of the more famous experiences recorded in the Gospels, Jesus Christ prayed in Gethsemane for the fortitude to make the last steps of

the journey to Calvary. Ellen White records the experience. "'If this cup may not pass away from Me, except I drink it, Thy will be done.' Three times has [Jesus] uttered that prayer. Three times has humanity shrunk from the last, crowning sacrifice. But now the history of the human race comes up before the world's Redeemer. He sees that the transgressors of the law, if left to themselves, must perish. He sees the helplessness of man. He sees the power of sin. . . . He will save man at any cost to Himself. He accepts His baptism of blood, that through Him perishing millions may gain everlasting life. He has left the courts of heaven, where all is purity, happiness, and glory, to save the one lost sheep, the one world that has fallen by transgression. And He will not turn from His mission. He will become the propitiation of a race that has willed to sin. His prayer now breathes only submission: 'If this cup may not pass away from Me, except I drink it, Thy will be done.' "[4]

Through the famous passage from Isaiah 53:11, the power of vision enabled Jesus Christ to persevere. At exactly the time when Christ needed endurance, the Word had testified 800 years earlier, "He shall see of the travail of his soul, and shall be satisfied."

7. **Vision elevates and blesses followers.** "Where there is no vision, the people perish" said Solomon in Proverbs 29:18. While the passage refers to prophetic vision, the principle is certainly true in all aspects of life—without vision, people, countries, companies, and organizations will spin into chaos. But where there is vision, the people will prosper. Consider the story of Joseph as an example of how vision can bless others through its power to shape leaders.

Vision, Suffering, and Leader-shaping

Joseph is one of my favorite figures in the entire Bible, because every experience of his life was leading him to be the leader that God wanted him to be. His early vision in Genesis 37 promised success, prominence, and rulership. But vision is no guarantee that we will not suffer. When sold into slavery at 17, Joseph could have in no way anticipated that enslavement, with its painful lessons, would be a part of God's plan for him. The Lord ultimately used his being a slave, with its forced discipline, as preparation for his future tasks, in which dutifulness, diligence, and dedication would catapult Joseph to the highest levels of Egyptian court life. Interestingly, every godly decision that Joseph makes in the Genesis narrative (see Gen. 37-41) seems to receive hardship and persecution as its reward.

His story occupies 13 of the last 14 chapters of the book of Genesis. He and his family take up the final third of this book of beginnings. In Genesis numerous personalities take the biblical stage and then step off of it—Adam, Eve, Noah, Enoch, Cain, Abraham, Isaac, Jacob, and Rebekah—each a luminary of Judeo-Christian history. By the time we get to chapter 39 of Genesis, however, it is all Joseph, all the time. I wonder if Moses, the writer of Genesis, was trying to tell us that Joseph is what servant leadership actually looks like across a whole life span, because he is one of the few leaders in the Bible of whom we get to scan God's workings across the whole chronology of his life. We meet him when he is finally born, after years of infertility, to Jacob's darling Rachel (see Gen. 30:22-24). Next we are with him when at 17 years of age he has his first vision (see Gen. 37), and finally we march out of Egypt with him as a part of his funeral train after his death at 110 years old (see Gen. 50). Before then we walk through the painful experiences that occur after his initial vision—betrayal by his brothers, being sold into slavery, being a blessing to Potiphar's household, being set up by Potiphar's desperate wife, watching when he's banished to prison, and then seeing the vision at last materialize at age 30, when Joseph becomes the prime minister of Egypt.

Now, here is the marvel of Joseph's life. Between the years of 30 and 110—for 80 years—Joseph remains loyal to his God and the divine vision for his life. It's one thing to be faithful in the midst of adversity. From ages 17 to 30 it would seem natural for him to pray, since it was his season of adversity. Who wouldn't do that while facing false accusations, going to trial, or being arraigned before a kangaroo court? But between ages 30 and 110 Joseph remains just as devoted to God in prosperity as he was in adversity.

God is in the leader-shaping business, and as leaders sometimes we need to step back and ask Him to help us to connect the dots of our experiences. Joseph was able to do that in Genesis 45:1-11 when he finally got to tell his brothers, "You sold me, but God sent me to Egypt to protect you" (see verse 5). In my duties as president of Oakwood University, I enjoy the privilege of working with many young people who do not have fathers. Once a week I have a student-only, no-appointment-needed visitation session called "Walk-up Wednesday." On that day Oakwood University students get to see the president without calling to make an appointment. As they come into my office they sometimes weep. The hole in their heart often leaves them asking God "Why?" They feel that He has abandoned them.

I can personally connect with such heart-heavy students, because I know what it feels like to be at school without an involved father. I know what it's like not to have the funds needed to finish. I know what it feels like—it's scary. Often you're wondering, *God, did You leave me too? My friends are going to laugh at me, saying, "We told you that you shouldn't have been going to Oakwood. Who do you think you are?"* But if God be for us, who can be against us? He is in the leader-shaping business and can use *all* of our experiences to move to us to where He wants us to be.

Where to Begin—Seeing Again

Now, fast-forward to a New Testament story about a blind man in the process of regaining his vision in Mark 10:45ff. Having fought through the opposition of the sighted but sightless crowd, blind Bartimaeus stands in the presence of Jesus in transparent openness. The servant Savior, who came not to be served but to serve, says to the man, "What would you like me to do for you?" He had asked the same question of the disciples in verse 36. When they had their opportunity, James and John requested power, position, and privilege. But listen to Bartimaeus.

He answers, "Lord, I want to see again." The word "Lord" is *Rabbounei* (Ραββουνει) in the Greek text, "my Master," a term of reverent respect. "I want to see again" is *anablepō* (ἀναβλεπω), "to recover sight." "My teacher, let me see again" (verse 51, NRSV). "Rabboni, *I want* to regain my sight" (verse 51, NASB). Here is where every leader has to begin—on his or her knees before God, requesting sight. If you have been jaded, or discouraged to the point that you may have lost your leadership vision, Jesus wants to restore it—He wants to help you see again!

Start by writing out your leadership vision statement. Below is a guide that I pray will assist you in becoming the leader that God wants you to be.

Elements of a Vision Statement

1. **Clarity.** A vision statement should look clearly into the future to describe the kind of organization that will successfully navigate the coming world.

2. **Potency.** A vision statement must command the follower's attention and imagination.
3. **Brevity.** A vision statement must be brief enough to be shared both within and beyond the organization.
4. **Stability.** A vision statement must stabilize the collective consciousness of the organization while engendering the hope and enthusiasm needed to face the uncertainties of the future.
5. **Desirability.** A vision statement must intersect with the aspirations of followers so that it expresses *their* hopes and dreams for the future well-being of the organization.
6. **Mutuality.** A vision must enlist others in a shared picture of an abundant and promising future.

May we each become the leaders that God has called us to be, by having a vision of His plans for our leadership and the followers entrusted to our care!

---

[1] John Kotter, "Leading Change: Why Transformation Efforts Fail," *Harvard Business Review,* March-April 1995.

[2] www.sermoncentral.com/illustrations/sermon-illustrations-david-school-stories-16517.asp.

[3] E. G. White, *The Ministry of Healing,* p. 500.

[4] E. G. White, *The Desire of Ages,* pp. 690, 691.

Chapter 10

THE LEADER'S PRIORITIES

Lowell C. Cooper

VICE PRESIDENT, GENERAL CONFERENCE OF SEVENTH-DAY ADVENTISTS

Accepting a position of leadership brings with it many surprises. It is particularly true for those entrusted with administrative responsibilities.

The unexpected comes quickly: 1. The increase in responsibility is accompanied by less ability to manage details. 2. Although you have authority, it can lead to unpleasant consequences when you use it. 3. You constantly need to make decisions even though you never have the time you would like to think through them. 4. You no longer seem to have any privacy, as others observe everything that you do and interpret it as an indicator of your leadership. 5. You suddenly discover you are really not the "boss". 6. Pleasing people is not the goal of leadership, as you have to deal with unpleasant tasks and convince people of the legitimacy of long-term views. 7. And finally, you realize that you are not God, as you get tired, find your wisdom insufficient, and make mistakes.

Welcome to leadership—and the need to set priorities. It is important to approach your daily tasks in order of importance. But the priority setting that we address here has little to do with the agenda for the day. Instead, it involves how you set the agenda for your life and the impact that it has on how you practice leadership.

We will consider five things that belong in the top tier of leadership priorities. They represent guiding concepts or principles more than specific leadership tasks. You can complete a task and turn to something else. But one does not complete a principle and then shift from it to address a different matter. Principles provide a framework within which leaders attend to their tasks.

The following five leadership priorities require careful reflection, deliberate decisions, and sustained commitment.

1. Building beneath the surface—the priority of character
2. Managing time—the priority of a balanced life
3. Serving with integrity—the priority of building trust
4. Working with partners—the priority of teamwork
5. Leaving a legacy—the priority of developing people

Building Beneath the Surface—The Priority of Character

The Brooklyn Bridge is a famous landmark spanning the East River in New York City. At the time it opened (1883) it was the largest suspension bridge in the world—50 percent longer than any previously built. For several years the towers were the tallest structures in the Western Hemisphere.

The strength and stability of the bridge depends much on the extensive steel, concrete, and masonry foundations for the two towers that carry the suspension cables for the bridge itself. Those massive structures are not visible, however. They lie beneath the surface of the water and, in fact, extend deep into the earth.

The tower foundations illustrate a truth about leadership: what is done inside the heart and mind, where people cannot see, determines whether a leader will stand the tests of time and circumstance. Only the inner life, which God alone sees, will inform, stabilize, and sustain—or weaken and corrode—the visible aspects of leadership. You accomplish such inner work through worship, devotion, prayer, and reflection about ethics, morals, and values.

Today one hears a lot about leadership strategy, leadership vision, and the marketing and communication of leadership ideas. The risk is that you may spend all your time on such leadership concepts and forget that character-building is your first priority.

Jesus spoke in graphic terms about the contrasts between the outer and the inner life (see Matt. 23:13-28). The outside of cup and platter may be so clean as to glisten in the sun, but the inside can remain full of corruption. Religious leaders might be as attractive as newly painted tombstones in a well-manicured cemetery, but the inviting exterior only hides inner decay. Such is the tragedy of leaders failing to recognize the importance of the inner life.

On another occasion Jesus spoke about the influence of one's life. "On the last day, that great day of the feast, Jesus stood and cried out, saying, 'If anyone thirsts, let him come to Me and drink. He who believes in Me, as the Scripture has said, out of his heart will flow rivers of living water'" (John 7:37, 38, NKJV).

What Jesus is saying is that if you want your life to be influential, the first thing is to make sure it is connected to the right source. Perhaps the leadership principle most important for spiritual leaders is that when you guard your secret life with God, your public life will take care of itself. Jesus assures us that if we are connected to Him, the visible effect of our lives, however small, will be a blessing to the world.

Far too often news headlines today describe the downfall of persons who have carried enormous responsibility and enjoyed public trust. And then to everyone's amazement the corroded inner life of such a leader gets exposed—perhaps through an act of financial fraud, failure to tell the truth in a moment of crisis, unfaithfulness to a spouse, or the cancerous effects of a private addiction. Leaders of religious organizations are not immune to public failure. The environment of power and the accolades of colleagues can easily blind a person to the risks that accompany position and prestige. It requires the inner life to anchor the public life.

How then do we attend to the inner life, the character-building work so essential to survival in public leadership? It happens primarily in what we do with our quiet time—those moments of the day reserved for feeding and focusing the mind. Those private periods when we wrestle with huge questions: What kind of person do I want to be? What kind of person am I called to be? For what purpose am I living? To whom do I turn for mentoring? What are the values by which I live?

It is a myth that a crisis develops character. It does not. Crisis reveals character. The urgent lesson for leaders is that during changing times—moments of crisis—strength comes from one's spiritual disciplines. Such habits do not develop on the spur of the moment. They yield their fruit only when carefully cultivated with consistency and honesty.

Ellen G. White cautioned and encouraged leaders that "it is not the capabilities you now possess, or ever will have, that will give you success. It is that which the Lord can do for you. . . . He longs to give you understanding in temporal as well as in spiritual matters. He can sharpen the intellect. He can give tact and skill. Put your talents into the work, ask God for wisdom, and it will be given you."[1]

Building beneath the surface is the most important work that any leader can do. Placing oneself in the presence of God, listening to His Word and seeking His counsel, will bring stability and strength to a leader's life. "The meek will he guide in judgment: and the meek will he teach his way" (Ps. 25:9).

Managing Time—The Priority of a Balanced Life

Time constraints and opportunities are universal. At some point or another, everyone faces time management issues.

Moses prayed, "Teach us to number our days, that we may gain a heart of wisdom" (Ps. 90:12, NIV).

Jesus and His disciples experienced the busyness of ministry. "Because so many people were coming and going that they did not even have a chance to eat, he said to them, 'Come with me by yourselves to a quiet place and get some rest'" (Mark 6:31, NIV).

Leaders must boldly and aggressively evaluate their use of time. The temptation occasionally arises to define oneself in terms of the office or responsibilities held. The result is to devote more and more time and energy to work. Eventually a person burns out, family relationships suffer, and health gets compromised.

Busyness viewed as a badge of importance is really a fraud. As Mary O'Connor observed: "It's not so much how busy you are, but why you are busy. The bee is praised; the mosquito is swatted."

Time management is somewhat of a myth, for we cannot create, expand, or stockpile time. When we talk about it, we are really speaking about managing ourselves. Time is a finite resource—there is no such thing as a longer hour or minute. Energy is a different story—it can be created, expanded, renewed, depleted, or lost.

Leveraging time is different from managing time. It means to achieve the most by focusing on what is of greatest importance and using efficient patterns of action to accomplish tasks. We learn to leverage time by taking a big-picture view, deciding what matters most, and then using efficient action to accomplish the task.

Managing time is a matter of discipline. It requires an action plan and firm resolve. But one must be careful about too much rigidity. Being too rigid can diminish satisfaction. Life consists of surprises, unpredictability, and attentiveness.

In a parable about the human condition of speed and inattention Søren Kierkegaard described a certain rich man who traveled in a finely appointed carriage, with lanterns on each corner of his vehicle to light the road around and ahead. He went his way in satisfaction and security, assured that his wealth provided him with a good life. One day along the road the rich man passed a poor peasant who had no carriage to carry him, no lamp to light his way. Yet while the rich man pitied the poor peasant who had no money to buy all the creature comforts, the poor peasant could see the stars, which the rich man missed because he was blinded by his lamps.

There is no one right formula for structuring a balanced life. Finding and celebrating the right relationship is more art than science, because time is measured not only by length but by quality. And the balance cannot be something static and inflexible. Nevertheless, we must always factor certain essential components into the harmonized life. They include personal time (for devotions, reflection, exercise, and proper nutrition); family and social time (for the nurture of relationships and mentoring of children); work time (for carrying out one's assigned responsibilities and earning a living); and rest time (including annual vacations, during which we take a larger block of time away from the regular routine of work and duty).

A balanced life creates, renews, and expands energy.

Serving With Integrity — The Priority of Building Trust

A basic task of leaders is to conduct their personal lives and public leadership in a manner that builds trust. They should remember that according to George MacDonald (1824-1905), "to be trusted is a greater compliment than to be loved."

Two kinds of trust impact a leader's life. The first is personal trust, what employees and church members have in individual leaders. While we judge ourselves by our intentions, others evaluate us by our actions. Building trust takes time and careful attention. A single action can instantly destroy it.

Questions of personal trust are as old as human community. Jacob cheated his brother, Esau. Laban defrauded his nephew Jacob. Critics of the apostle Paul insinuated doubts about his integrity. He responded with a statement about the authenticity of his life: "We have renounced secret and shameful ways; we do not use deception, nor do we distort the word of God. On the contrary, by setting forth the truth plainly we commend ourselves to every man's conscience in the sight of God" (2 Cor. 4:2, NIV).

An overwhelming awareness that God had called Paul governed the complexities of his ethical and moral decision-making. Through God's mercy he had received a work to do. That conviction became his central reference point.

Paul asserts that the disciplinary code for his life is an internal one, not the result of external rules, guidelines, policies, audits, or outside supervision. The realization that his ministry comes by the grace of God compels him to live a life of integrity. Basing his behavior on the privilege of being associated with God's program for the world, he declared that "we live in such a way that no one will stumble because of us, and no one will find fault with our ministry" (2 Cor. 6:3, NLT).

The development of trust toward someone in leadership has its origin in the interplay of character and competence. Leaders with upright character but who lack competence do not inspire confidence. Similarly, those with obvious qualifications but with questionable character will lack credibility. Character and competence teamed together create a solid foundation for the growth of trust.

Stephen M. R. Covey writes about the loss and restoration of trust in leadership. "Generally, the quickest way to decrease trust is to violate a behavior of character, while the quickest way to increase trust is to demonstrate a behavior of competence."[2]

The second kind of trust concerns confidence in the organization, the firm conviction that an organization's purposes are valid and its operations will be consistent with its policies and public statements. Besides living in a way that builds personal trust, leaders in the church must also function in a manner that generates confidence in it as an institution.

This is one of the most important global leadership tasks in the Seventh-day Adventist Church. For the reality is that mistakes and failures occurring in one place can be, and usually are, communicated instantly to many other locations around the world. An attitude of distrust focused on a particular denominational unit can quickly metastasize into a generalized distrust of the whole organization. It is especially true in the areas of employment practices and management of church funds, the tithes and offerings made available to it as an expression of the members' stewardship.

Working With Partners—The Priority of Teamwork

Zeal and energy are wonderful characteristics in employees. But unless accompanied by a grasp of where our roles fit into the larger organizational mission and structure, they can cause definite damage to the institution as well as to our colleagues. So before we as leaders dive into our work it is necessary to know what is expected of us, what is the organizational structure within which we perform, how we relate to others, and how collaboration happens.

It seems so mundane to suggest that people carefully study the mission statement of the organization they serve, the organizational structure, the culture of the organization, and the specific job description for their position. To do so demands more than a cursory reading of some dry policy documents, even though that is where you will find the information.

Understanding such things takes time and attention. The degree to which we can contribute to the mission and progress of an organization depends largely on how well we comprehend such matters. In organizational life "no man is an island."

Certainly within the Seventh-day Adventist Church any leader who believes that they are at the center with everything else revolving around them is headed for failure. Whatever leadership role we have is intricately connected to many other roles filled by other people. Effective leadership requires a team consciousness, not a hero mentality.

"Let not one man feel that his gift alone is sufficient for the work of God; that he alone can carry through a series of meetings, and give perfection to the work. His methods may be good, and yet varied gifts are essential; one man's mind is not to mold and fashion the work according to his special ideas. . . . Cooperation and unity are essential to a harmonious whole, each laborer doing his God-given work, filling his appropriate position, and supplying the deficiency of another. One worker left to labor alone is in danger of thinking that his talent is sufficient to make a complete whole."[3]

The challenge of teamwork is to create a partnership that is complementary, productive, effective, and satisfying. Self-centered people cannot function well in a team.

A person with team consciousness recognizes that:
- every position is necessary
- each position has a specialized function
- each participant must know the rules and procedures

- team members must be in constant communication
- each team member does their best when there is mutual support and cooperation

And further, the test of a group becoming a team is passed when each member of the team is sufficiently confident of themselves and their contribution so as to praise the skills of the others. Building teams and working in partnerships is a leadership priority.

Paul, in 1 Corinthians 12, compares the church, composed of many members, with a body and its various parts. Eugene Peterson's translation *The Message* captures important insights for all leaders:

"I want you to think about how all this makes you more significant, not less. A body isn't just a single part blown up into something huge. It's all the different-but-similar parts arranged and functioning together.... But I also want you to think about how this keeps your significance from getting blown up into self-importance. For no matter how significant you are it is only because of what you are a *part* of. An enormous eye or a gigantic hand wouldn't be a body, but a monster" (1 Cor. 12:12-23, Message).

Leaving a Legacy—The Priority of Developing People

Another top leadership priority is to think about what a person will leave when they quit the job or retire. Leadership is not just a matter of seeing what can be done today. It is also about preparing people and the organization for the future.

The responsibilities one carries today will shift to the shoulders of another tomorrow. Every leader, whether an administrator or not, needs to be intentional about passing the torch to a succeeding generation. It involves helping to equip people with skills, engaging their creativity and commitment, enabling them to comprehend and embrace the mission of the organization, and teaching them the art of leadership.

To the extent that we want power we are in the flesh, and the Holy Spirit has no part in us. Christ put a towel around Himself and washed His disciples' feet. We should ask ourselves from time to time, "Whose feet am I washing?"[4]

The life of Barnabas, seen through the brief glimpses recorded in the book of Acts, is a powerful example of a leader who left a legacy. He appears on the scene (see Acts 4:36) as a person of integrity. In contrast to Ananias and Sapphira, he keeps his promises. When the disciples were wary about accepting the now-converted Paul, he demonstrated great personal risk by encouraging Paul and convincing the disciples of Paul's authentic spiritual experience (see Acts 9:26-30).

In Antioch, a place where a church was planted without official sanction by and involvement of the "accepted" leaders, Barnabas saw the grace of God (see Acts 11:19-24) rather than the weaknesses and mistakes of the fledgling congregation. Remaining in Antioch, seeing the needs there, and perhaps recognizing his own limitations, he invites Paul to join him in the work (see verses 25, 26). Barnabas recognized talent and ability and was big enough to bring other gifted people into leadership.

The last we learn about Barnabas is the separation from Paul as a result of a disagreement about the presence of young John Mark (see Acts 15:36-41). On a previous journey John Mark had not measured up to Paul's expectations. The apostle did not want to be burdened with him now. It led to a sharp division with Barnabas and finally to the breakup of the dynamic team. Paul took Silas while Barnabas accepted John Mark.

The incident removed Barnabas from history's limelight. We do not know much more about him. Did he sacrifice his own career for Mark? But what we do know is that, later on, Paul once again found Mark a valuable companion (see Col. 4:10 and 2 Tim. 4:11). Would the story have ended differently if Barnabas had not dedicated himself to the nurture of Mark?

Barnabas was focused, not on making a name for himself, but in leaving a legacy of persons devoted to and engaged in the great mission of God.

Conclusion

Any leader with experience knows the value of setting priorities in the daily agenda. It is even more vital for them to understand the importance of setting priorities about life. For it is when life's priorities are firmly embraced that the role of leadership becomes effective.

---

[1] E. G. White, *Christ's Object Lessons,* p. 146.

[2] Stephen M. R. Covey, *The Speed of Trust* (New York: Free Press), p. 133.

[3] Ellen G. White, *Evangelism* (Washington, D.C.: Review and Herald Pub. Assn., 1946), p. 104.

[4] Francis A. Schaeffer, *No Little People* (Downers Grove, Ill.: InterVarsity Press, 1974), p. 68.

Chapter 11

THE LEADER'S FIRST STEPS

Gordon Bietz

PRESIDENT, SOUTHERN ADVENTIST UNIVERSITY

I was the newly minted president of the Georgia-Cumberland Conference. It was my first Sabbath appointment, and I was scheduled to offer the dedication prayer at the Jasper Seventh-day Adventist Church. My wife and I rose early to make the one-hour drive to the church from our home in Collegedale, Tennessee. We arrived well before the 9:30 a.m. Sabbath school, and my first impression was that the congregation had not planned anything particularly special for that day. I met the pastor, who seemed perplexed and surprised to see the new conference president at his church. A few phone calls later I became aware of the fact that I had driven to Jasper, Tennessee, instead of Georgia, the site of the special service. Two hours later we arrived at the Georgia church in time for the potluck, much to my embarrassment and the amusement of the congregation, particularly the conference officers who attended the special service.

It was not an auspicious beginning to my administration of the conference, but it did give me an opportunity to exhibit a couple of traits of good leadership: humility and humor. The following week at the conference office morning worship the staff had a great time providing me with maps of the conference territory and making me the butt of more jokes than I can remember. It was all great fun, and it gave me opportunity to show my sense of humor and portray humility. Obviously I hadn't come to the conference presidency with all the answers.

Some studies indicate that we judge a person within the first seven seconds of meeting them. First impressions are lasting ones. The first talk the leader presents to the staff, the first committee they chair, and the first sermon given at the new church assignment—all of those "firsts" provide an opportunity to set the tone of their leadership. You don't have a second chance to make a first impression.

Some other things I did communicated the tone I wanted to set at the beginning of my service at the Georgia-Cumberland Conference. I removed the designated parking space for the president. Since anyone in that position travels a lot, for the president to have the best parking space seemed elitist. I feel in my heart a sense of equality with everyone I work with. We have different gifts, and even though my gifts have brought me to the office of president, that doesn't make them any better than the ones that have brought my secretary to her vocation.

The second thing I did early on in my role was to meet individually with all of the secretaries in the office. I didn't first consult with the departmental heads or vice presidents, but with the secretaries. In many very practical ways they are the ones who not only run the nuts and bolts of the office operations but also know about what works and what doesn't. The significance of meeting early on with them communicated how I valued them and their work.

In the same way, when I came to pastor the Collegedale, Tennessee, church, my first duty was to meet with all of the elders in their homes. The congregation was too large to visit all of the members, but connecting with the local leadership in a personal way filtered to the rest of the congregation. Leadership grows from relationships, and establishing good relationships right from the beginning is vitally important.

Anyone who accepts a position of leadership faces the danger of thinking that they have received a mantle of authority or power. Being chosen to be a leader only gives people the opportunity to demonstrate leadership—it doesn't automatically make anyone a leader. Positional leadership is not real leadership. It is only when people choose to follow you out of their free will that you are really leading.

Some years later the board of trustees of Southern Adventist University offered me its presidency, and in the process of determining if I should accept the position, I requested a general meeting with the entire faculty. I had an open question-and-answer session with them and then asked them to vote by secret ballot whether I should accept the position or not. I determined before the vote that the faculty would decide whether I would take the job. Leadership is granted by those who follow—not by the board of trustees. As someone said: "If you think you are leading and no one is following, you are only taking a walk."

I believe what John Maxwell says: "Leadership is influence" and "People buy into the leader before they buy into the vision." When you are new in a position, your influence is limited, because you don't have the relationships with the people you seek to influence. That is why your first actions are so important: they set the stage for your leadership. They give the first impression of who you are as a person. It is important to remember that leaders don't do the work. The work of the organization is done by the people who are led. If they don't respect, appreciate, and like the leader, he or she will have no influence over them. They may put in the time to get a paycheck, but their creative energy won't be fully tapped into.

Everyone is a leader, because everyone has a circle of influence. Whether the elder, pastor, janitor, secretary, deacon, or church member, everyone influences the organization. All bring their ideas and their baggage to the table as the entity seeks to move into the future. The designated leader (be they pastor or president, department chair or dean) is to use their gifts to bring the diverse elements in the organization to focus on the direction of its mission.

At the beginning of the new leader's responsibilities it is important to do a lot of listening. Leaders need to know what is on the hearts and minds of those they are working with, and that doesn't happen without being willing to hear what others have to say. At the beginning of a leader's tenure (and occasionally throughout it) they should take the time to go to each department in the organization and simply say, "Tell me about your department and your vision for it going forward." It is a question you ask not because you plan to micromanage that department, but only to get a feel for its activity and vision.

Management by walking around (MBWA) is important anytime but particularly in the early days of a new position as the leader takes time to make informal visits to work areas and listen to the employees. It keeps one's finger on the pulse of the organization. I learn a great deal by this informal approach, and people tend to open up and share a lot of useful information that contributes to decisions I make in more formal settings.

Decisions that you make early in an administration communicate the direction you would like to see the organization head. Will you be spending money to fix up your office? Or will you be using it to make the work of others easier? As leaders we are not emptiness to be filled with the external symbols of success, but rather we are fullness to be emptied in service to others. We should exemplify servant leadership.

Jesus demonstrated the ultimate example of servant leadership. He came not to show off His worth but rather to give us worth. Our Savior did not enrich Himself at our expense but rather impoverished Himself to make us rich. And He did not seek to impress us with His glory but rather to share His glory with us. And so as leaders demonstrate to those who follow that they have the best interest of the latter in their heart, they will have influence—not positional influence but, more important, relational influence.

The most important first step in a new position is to develop a relationship with those you will be serving. What are their needs? What is their vision for the organization? What are they passionate about? What diminishes their enthusiasm? Relational leadership means that it is out of those human, personal-level connections that you influence the organization.

One danger new leaders face is to have a sense of aggrandizement, of feeling somehow that their newly granted position gives them some kind of power over other people. As previously suggested, the position provides only the opportunity to demonstrate whether or not you are a leader. Unfortunately, some use the opportunity of a new position to feed their ego rather than to serve others.

Many are the ways that you can subliminally communicate the message that now that you have this position you are better than others, that you were chosen and others were not, and that you were elevated and the others were not. You can create that impression by the way you spend money, by expressing opinions on committees and elsewhere as if they were the last word, and by expecting to be treated differently than others.

The people exist in an organization not to serve you, but for you as the leader to serve them. Successful leadership is serving others to enable them to reach their goals rather than feeding on others so that you can reach your goals.

When I started as president of the Georgia-Cumberland Conference, I had been a pastor for 25 years and knew pretty much how things operated. Then I accepted the position of president of Southern Adventist University, and I remember my first day at work as its president. I walked down the hall and saw my name on the door, "Gordon Bietz, President," and thought to myself, *What have I done? I don't have a clue about how to run a university.* And as it turned out, that was my salvation, because I didn't need to operate the university—I just had to know how to work with the team that was actually running the university. I just needed to trust them and encourage them to continue their work. Leadership is not about having all the answers, but surrounding yourself with people who have the answers and then giving them the support they require to do their work.

The new leader must not succumb to the attitude of James and John as expressed by their mother to Jesus: "In your Kingdom, please let my two sons sit in places of honor next to you, one on your right and the other on your left" (Matt. 20:21, NLT). The human heart has an insatiable desire to be honored and the constant feeling that a certain position will provide that honor. We live in a world of competition in which the winners get positions of honor and the losers don't.

Unfortunately, too many of us have bought into society's value formula of success. But we need to accept the value formula of Jesus: "Among you it will be different. Whoever wants to be a leader among you must be your servant, and whoever wants to be first among you must become your slave. For even the Son of Man came not to be served but to serve others and to give his life as a ransom for many" (verses 26-28, NLT).

Chapter 12

THE LEADER'S DISCIPLINE

Lilya Wagner

DIRECTOR, NORTH AMERICAN DIVISION PHILANTHROPIC SERVICE FOR INSTITUTIONS

with **Halvard Thomsen**

ASSISTANT TO THE PRESIDENT, NORTH AMERICAN DIVISION

More than 200 years ago United States president Thomas Jefferson asked Meriwether Lewis to see if there existed an all-river route from the Mississippi River to the Pacific Ocean. At that time no one knew exactly how far the continent stretched or what type of terrain existed in the wilderness. Lewis chose his Army buddy William Clark as his second-in-command. Both were in their early 30s. They set out in 1804 with more than 30 adventurers. Lewis had been not only a soldier but also a plantation owner and a personal aide to President Jefferson, who had spotted the young man's leadership characteristics and charisma. Both Lewis and Clark exhibited disciplined leadership skills in accomplishing a bold and useful task.

Having to explore and chart unmapped territory, Lewis spent two years acquiring the scientific skills in order to do so. Beyond that, they had to be optimistic, especially around others. They faced physical and emotional stress during the expedition. The physical exertion alone would have strained the limits of any human.

In addition, they had to be courageous, not foolhardy. While they took risks, they did so intelligently. Instead of attacking Native American tribes who were hostile, they learned to coexist. They never allowed pride to overshadow good judgment, and they remained focused on the enterprise at hand.

Above all, they were honest and objective. Jefferson said Lewis had "a fidelity to truth so scrupulous that whatever he should report would be certain as if seen by ourselves."[1]

More than 3,000 years before Lewis and Clark a well-disciplined leader rose from a most unlikely place. Eleventh of the 12 sons of Jacob, Joseph seemed to exhibit little or no discipline as a young man and certainly no leadership. His brothers scoffed when he told his dreams suggesting a role as leader. But we begin to get a hint of his discipline when as a slave he resisted the seductive proposition of his master's wife, even though prison was his reward. Perhaps it was the stories about Great-grandfather Abraham that he heard again and again from his father that gave him the foundation for fidelity to God and enabled him to develop the discipline that equipped him for leadership. The account of Joseph's faithfulness to even the smallest duty and positive attitude in face of unjust incarceration reached Pharaoh, who quickly recognized his value as a wise leader.

Like Lewis and Clark, Joseph took calculated and courageous risks as he taxed the people for seven years to fill the storehouses. He modeled self-control to preserve the resources of his adopted nation during a time of plenty, when it would have been easier to squander them. We also see that self-control—discipline—in his dealings with his brothers when he restrained his emotions, withholding his identity until the right moment.

These individuals selected from both secular and spiritual history exemplify some of the traits that might define discipline in practicing leadership. By studying what made them so outstanding we can begin to find out what it means to be a disciplined leader. The word *discipline* can be problematic if we don't determine how it is used in a particular context. For example, "to be disciplined" might mean that someone is punishing us. To lead with discipline might, in turn, imply that we are controlling or punishing someone else. Therefore, we need to define the leader's discipline, the focus of this chapter.

We believe that leadership is a conscious decision based on spiritual, ethical, and moral values. It is a commitment to behaviors that result in performance according to the highest religious and professional standards. Therefore, disciplined leadership is both an attitude and a resulting set of behaviors and actions that can be measured and that are clear, organized, and capable of being implemented. Disciplined leadership involves emotions, relationships, achievements, and integrity, as illustrated below.

We have selected these four characteristics as the most essential in the leader's discipline. We begin with the emotions and work our way around the illustration until we reach the most cerebral aspect of leadership.

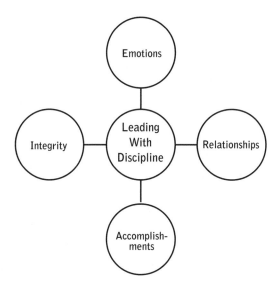

Emotions

During His time on earth, people often questioned, ridiculed, defamed, and reviled Jesus. He could easily have brought down fire from heaven, as His disciples urged, to punish or annihilate His persecutors, but He chose to exhibit the utmost discipline in how He related to such annoyances and hurts. Jesus remained calm even though He could no doubt see right through the motives and intentions of those who tried to trip Him up with their emotion-charged questions and accusations. Watch Him calmly face the crafty plot of the Pharisees as they seek to trap Him: "Is it lawful to pay taxes to the emperor, or not?" Unfazed and in perfect control of His emotions, Jesus knocks His foes off balance with His first words, "Show me the coin used for the tax" (Matt. 22:17, 19, NRSV). Jesus maintained His dignity. Refusing to allow Himself to stoop to the level of His accusers, He didn't give way to anger, which would have denigrated Him in the eyes of His followers as well as His tormentors.

Caring for others through genuine compassion, Jesus avoided false and excessive emotion while approaching their needs in just the appropriate ways. He put His concern into disciplined action, such as when He fed the 5,000 and managed that complex event with both personal as well as organizational discipline. Jesus focused on the needs of others and was not self-centered. When He showed emotion, it was because of His compassion, and He put that compassion into action. His unselfishness showed in the smallest actions, such as comforting the widow of Nain, and culminated in the greatest one of all—giving His life for us. What discipline it took to lead the sinful world toward an eternal hope!

We see such examples from the life of Jesus also emulated by notable figures in human history who have left an indelible mark on how we view the leader's discipline in practice. For example, the heroic pioneer missionary in Africa, Albert Schweitzer, went to Africa in 1913 because he saw a great need. While working with uncommon zeal and compassion, he also maintained a discipline in how he led the medical program, and at the same time took the time to improve himself and leave a legacy in another way as well. He produced what even today is considered the best editions of Johann Sebastian Bach's organ works. Although he could easily have given in to fatigue at the end of the day and relaxed in the shade of his veranda, he chose to provide an enormous service for his present-day environment and care for needs, while also benefiting a defined population of musical performers for years to come.

True greatness, as exemplified so remarkably by the life of Dr. Schweitzer, who as a theologian, organist, philosopher, physician, and medical missionary transcends the restrictions of time and popular opinion, emanates from genuine humility. It displays a self-assuredness that comes from a person's ability to do what might otherwise be more enjoyable to postpone, to take thoughtful action when a lazy mind might be more comfortable, and to achieve results instead of sitting on the sidelines.

During the Cultural Revolution in China the government imprisoned many extraordinarily talented leaders in the arts and sciences. One was a renowned pianist. While he languished in his cell, he continued to practice his music in his head as well as exercise his fingers in every way possible. When released, he walked to his beloved piano and executed a Mozart sonata with skill that surpassed even his preincarceration performances. Such was the power of his disciplined mind and emotions that he rose above the indignity of unfair and brutal imprisonment and emerged as an even stronger leader in his field and in his country.

Relationships

In considering the discipline of emotions, we have progressed to the next quality of a leader's discipline, and perhaps have unwittingly illustrated the strong connection between the discipline of emotions and relationships. To lead with discipline in relationships is to treat employees, colleagues, acquaintances, church members—everyone in our particular world—with courtesy, respect, and appreciation. Often we consider that which is different from our own environment and perspective as suspect and perhaps of little worth. But a disciplined leader respects and values differences as well as the commonalities that bind us together. Instead of seeing cultural, ethnic, experiential, and other characteristics as threats, such leaders use them to enhance their effectiveness in leadership.

Relationships with a leader's constituents are particularly significant, because through the leader's actions, they form a view or perception of the organization that they represent. The disciplined leader is friendly while maintaining dignity. In short, a disciplined leader is one whom others want to follow, not one who pushes from behind.

The ultimate relationship, however, is a disciplined leader's connection with God. In both Joseph and Jesus we see how a relationship with God—cultivated through discipline—provided a sense of identity and strength of character. It enabled them to relate to friend and foe with composure and respect, and raised them above their contemporaries. This relationship enabled them to inspire others to follow their lead.

Accomplishments

The disciplined leader always exerts his or her best effort in learning to do something well. The great violinist Mischa Dichter was once walking on the streets of New York when a man approached him and asked, "How do I reach Carnegie Hall?" With a sigh Dichter replied, "Practice, practice, practice!" Leading with discipline means doing the best job possible, not doing just enough to get by.

The discipline of accomplishment includes having a sense of timeliness—as Ecclesiastes notes, there is a time for everything. Controlling one's thoughts and speaking one's mind at the correct time and in the right way involves much self-discipline and careful attention, but results in credibility and respect.

The disciplined leader will always shun putting off anything that needs to be done. Admittedly, that is easier for some personality types than others, but all human beings are capable of developing such a trait. Delayed gratification may be necessary when leading with discipline. In addition, the disciplined leader pays attention to detail while not missing the big picture. Decisive action is a hallmark of such leaders, with thoughtful preparation leading to reasoned action.

The annals of human accomplishment, if we were to view them as a wall of honor in some imagined center of leadership excellence, would include an amazing array of achievements, but most, if not all, represented on that imaginary wall would state unequivocally that the path toward being honored included disciplined action.

Few lives in the secular arena display more historical significance than that of Queen Elizabeth I, who reigned in the late sixteenth and early seventeenth centuries. She was a crafty ruler whose reign saw triumphs from literature (Shakespeare) to war (the Spanish Armada). The life of Queen Elizabeth has much to say about the leader's discipline. According to *Elizabeth I, CEO: Strategic Lessons From the Leader Who Built an Empire,* by Alan Axelrod, the queen's long reign offers numerous lessons in leadership. Elizabeth treated England as a dynamic system based, perhaps, on certain unchanging, transcendent principles, but she was always responsive to the circumstances of a fluid world. Although she faced grave dangers, formidable challenges, and spectacular opportunities, she still managed them both to her advantage and to that of England. An exceptional administrator, she knew how to develop a leadership image, communicate effectively, establish priorities, inspire others, create loyalty and build a team, be an effective mentor, inspire maximum performance, and cultivate exceptional quality.[2]

Among the biblical heroes on our wall of honor would be Queen Esther, who accomplished the incredible feat of saving an entire population because she had courage to face down an unprincipled and undisciplined leader. She used her exalted position wisely and for the benefit of others while subsuming ego.

Integrity

This brings us to the last characteristic we will consider: leading with integrity. Disciplined administrators always engage in ethical behavior. They make the right choice whether or not it's the popular or accepted thing to do. Ethical behavior means doing what's proper even when no one is watching. A landmark document produced by Independent Sector, the leading coalition of nonprofits, foundations, and corporate giving programs committed to advancing the common good in America, *Obedience to the Unenforceable*, perhaps expresses it best. Of all the traits essential to the leader's discipline, it regards integrity as of top priority. We could regard leading with integrity as the benchmark to measure all other disciplined behavior against, whether in accomplishments, relationships, or emotions. While "gray areas" will continue to exist, disciplined leaders can validate the choices they make because they have trained their minds to think rationally while not forgetting sensitivity and feeling.

How disciplined are you as a leader? We don't suggest that you must be rigid, static, or inflexible. However, a framework of discipline is essential for effective leaders—those who do what others shun or are not willing to do. Discipline is the only lasting remedy to today's environment of massive interruptions to our ability to work on what matters most. Disciplined leaders focus on a personal strategy that involves emotional intelligence and maturity. They form relationships based on respect and dignity while not forgetting an essential sense of caring, and they avoid those interruptions that hinder the ability to work on that which matters most, whether professional, personal, or spiritual.

Jim Collins, writing in the *Harvard Business Review*, discussed level 5 leaders and how necessary they are to organizational change and good leadership. Administrators at that level have the ability to build enduring greatness through a paradoxical combination of personal humility plus professional will. As Collins says, level 5 leadership is essential for taking an organization from good to great. Such leaders maintain the belief that they can surmount obstacles and prevail at the end. They understand that transformations do not happen overnight but in incremental steps. And level 5 leaders are disciplined in thought and action. What lies at the heart of this theory is that level 5 characteristics—of moving from good to great—can be in most of us if we practice leading with discipline.[3]

In summary, we refer once again to the graphic of four essential traits necessary to achieve the leader's discipline, and list the key points in the natural flow from disciplined emotions to disciplined and ethical accomplishment:

- Remain calm.
- Maintain dignity.
- Care for others with genuine compassion.
- Focus on the needs of others.

- Treat all with courtesy, respect, and appreciation.
- Value differences.
- Maintain a balance in rational thought and feeling.
- Emanate genuine humility.
- Be justifiably self-assured.
- Be someone whom others want to follow, not one who pushes from behind.
- Exert your best effort in doing something well.
- Achieve a sense of timeliness.
- Pay attention to detail while not missing the big picture.
- Take decisive action.
- Engage in ethical behavior.
- Validate choices made through rational thought while not forgetting sensitivity and feeling.
- Keep your word.

---

[1] Stephen Ambrose, *Undaunted Courage: Meriwether Lewis, Thomas Jefferson, and the Opening of the West* (New York: Simon and Schuster, 1996), p. 484.

[2] Alan Axelrod, *Elizabeth I, CEO: Strategic Lessons From the Leader Who Built an Empire* (Paramus, N.J.: Prentice Hall, 2000).

[3] Jim Collins, "Level 5 Leadership: The Triumph of Humility and Fierce Resolve," *Harvard Business Review,* January 2001, p. 70.

Chapter 13

The Leader's Courage

Jim Gilley

PRESIDENT AND CEO, THREE ANGELS BROADCASTING NETWORK

Leaders come in all sizes and body types as well as shapes and weights. They may be skinny or fat, tall or short, totally unattractive or extremely handsome. And they may be male or female. But if they are successful, they will understand one fundamental principle: leaders have followers.

You may be given a position as head of an organization, but you are not the leader until the right people in that organization follow you.

A number of years ago my son's sixth-grade teacher taught me this principle. We were talking about my eldest, Jim junior, and the man described him as a leader. "A leader?" I said incredulously. "That skinny kid?" I had never thought of him as a leader.

"You know how to tell a leader, don't you?" he asked. At this point I was silent. "A leader has followers," he explained, "and Jimmy has followers."

That teacher was right. Jimmy has served as CEO of several medical organizations since shortly after graduating from college—and he still has followers.

Very simple, but profound. You may think that you are leading, but if no one is following, then you are sadly mistaken. I have observed leadership for many years now, first in ministry and then for 25 years in private business. In ministry I served on the local church level as both a pastor and as a lay member of a church board. On the conference level I was a lay member of the conference executive committee, a departmental director, and a conference president.

During those years I have watched people who thought they were leading an organization but did not realize that no one was following at all. The lone wolf leader is a thing of the past. Now and then you will find entrepreneurs who run everything from the top to the bottom of the organization, but when it gets too large for one person to handle, they either turn it over to someone else to manage or they sell it off to start a new project.

Most church administrators are not entrepreneurs. If they were, they would quickly become frustrated with the process it takes to lead a church entity and would soon leave to start their own ministry, etc. To try to explain the leadership concept I have found that works within the church, I will bounce around between local church and conference—starting first at the congregational level.

Just because the conference has hired you to be the pastor doesn't mean that you are automatically the leader. If you are wise, you will spend your first few months getting acquainted and figuring out who the real leader of the church is. It may or may not be the head elder, it may be his wife, or it could be someone who doesn't even hold an office (and perhaps for some reason is even ineligible to hold one). It definitely is not the person who gives you the rush when you first arrive and tries to impress you and be your "new best friend."

Preaching the Word is vital. A pastor who "rightly divides the Word" in an interesting manner will win more support than in any other way. Make appointments and visit as many members in their homes as you can. If not, see them at the church. Visit your elders first, beginning with the head elder. Listen carefully and observe whom they talk to when they believe an important decision is to be made—it may be their spouse. The matriarch of the church leads more congregations than many may suppose, and in many cases rightly so. They may guide without holding any office at all.

When you find out who the true leader of the congregation is, spend a lot of time with that person. "Pick their brain," finding out what their vision for the church is and began to share your own vision slowly with, "What do you think about this?" Win them to your point of view. If you do, leading the church into the future will be much easier with the support of the local "natural" leader. It will make you as the pastoral leader much more successful. Furthermore, you will have a larger degree of peace in the church and greater success if you resist launching your own plans until you have tested the waters.

The "natural leader" may not even think of themselves as such. But one thing you will notice: when they express an opinion, people listen. What was the name of that brokerage firm people listened to? E. F. Hutton? Perhaps that was just an advertising slogan, but the "natural leader" will be there long after you have gone on to other things. That is, if you learn to work with them!

As you move into your second year, if at all possible make the "natural" leader your head elder, if they are not already in that position. I was fortunate that when I went to Arlington, Texas, the head elder was the natural leader of the church. If such an individual is not in this position, it creates a division that is hard to work with. I have seen pastors who resist the natural leader and either try to neutralize them or try to run them off. I would never be comfortable with that strategy. My method is to work closely with such a leader. Prayerfully become a team, and if that is not possible, "shake the dust from your feet" and look for another place to minister. "Where you work is not nearly as important as with whom you work" is a vital principle that I learned from a very successful leader.

My seven years in Arlington as a $1-a-year, full-time senior pastor who was running a business full time were some of the happiest years of my life. Arlington grew from fewer than 300 members to a few more than 1,000 during that time. The harmony between the pastoral team, who included my associate pastor, Henry Barron, and the lay leadership was truly amazing, and God honored it with growth. I believe the Lord leads people to a congregation that He can trust us with, and that the Holy Spirit guides us into the "unity of the truth" that will always result in success.

The same principles of leadership apply at the conference level as well. When I was called to be president of the Arkansas-Louisiana Conference I had a lot more to learn about leadership. Two weeks into my presidency the conference committee voted me out of office by a vote of 9-7, because they said that the union president who had chaired the nominating committee had used undue pressure. After I had experienced two months of devastating humiliation, the conference constituency committee appointed to elect a new president, in an action that surprised everyone (and none more than me), restored me as president. What a rocky start! Church historians tell me they know of no other time that such a thing has happened in the history of our denomination. (I would just as soon not have made history!)

Both my fellow officers—the secretary and the treasurer—had voted against me, as well as half of the rest of the conference committee. That first year was very difficult. It took most of that time to get us three officers working as a team. Those on the committee who had voted for me were the salt of the earth but were not the lay leaders of that committee. Although the latter had voted against me, I began to work to develop their confidence. Within a year both the officers and the lay leaders were working as a team. Wonderful things happened the next six years because of harmonious teamwork.

In building a successful conference team, it is important to begin with the other officers, particularly the secretary and the treasurer. Then one must gain the confidence of the conference committee. Beyond that, one must visit the churches to become aware of local challenges and opportunities and get to know the membership conference-wide. Success brings greater confidence and more success. But it cannot happen without constant communication. Returning phone calls and answering letters and e-mails swiftly pays big dividends, even if it is only an acknowledgment that you received their message and will look into it. A log of all phone calls, e-mails, and letters is vital. Include a response area on it so that you can later look back at what you advised, suggested, or promised.

Careful planning and preparation is absolutely necessary, especially before the conference committee meetings. Our conference committee met on Thursdays every other month. On Monday of that week we finalized the agenda. Then all three officers spent as much time as needed on Monday and Tuesday going over it and discussing each point. I wanted to make sure that we three were in complete agreement on each item. If we found ourselves with different opinions on something, we would talk about it until we came to a consensus. But if we couldn't (which was rare), we would withdraw the item from the agenda until we had more information to make our decision.

At times we might even present the item for discussion and ask the committee either to give the administrative committee (the three officers in an official meeting) the authority to make the final decision or to decide if it could wait until we brought a recommendation to the next committee. We would never under any circumstance disagree with one another during committee meetings (in private, yes, and often).

Nothing makes a conference committee more insecure than to have the leaders involved in heated disagreements during a constituency session. I've seen it happen a number of times, but nothing like I experienced years ago when I was a lay member of the Texas Conference executive committee. The president had been elected midterm. The secretary, a prince of a man, had then been handpicked by the new president. The president then insisted that the committee next appoint a treasurer who currently worked some distance away and who also had a number of difficulties. Unfortunately, the conference president soon found that he could not get along with either the secretary or the treasurer, and the disagreements began. That committee met every month, and it seemed that that was the only time they spoke to each other, and then in quite heated terms. Eventually church members at the constituency session voted all three out in what was the most terrible meeting I have ever attended. I liked all three men very much and really enjoyed working with them. All had fabulous ideas and plans, but never the same opinion.

A conference team that doesn't work together is doomed to failure. Word soon leaks out of the office into the field. Both the conference employees and the members develop an insecure feeling toward leadership, and it expresses itself when constituency time arrives.

Leadership brings about many joys and disappointments. During my first year as a conference president I faced so many difficulties that I thought anyone would have to be certified insane to want the job. I still think that it is a position that should seek you and never the opposite. In time I became more relaxed with the job, but I do believe it is the most challenging of all elected posts in the Seventh-day Adventist Church. Later I found myself chosen to be vice president of the North American Division. In comparison, that was a piece of cake. Don Schneider, at that time the division president, who had been president of five conferences and a union conference, told me that being a conference president was the most difficult position he had held.

The most exciting and rewarding position of leadership that I have ever had is my current one of president/CEO of Three Angels Broadcasting Network. As I have used the same team strategies here as I did at the conference level, I have found that they have produced similar results. I am surrounded by excellent people, and they could not be more cooperative.

Because of its extreme challenges, leadership can completely absorb the individual involved. Be careful not to fall into that trap. Keep your life balanced. Do not neglect any aspect of it. Always seek to maintain a proper relationship between the spiritual, family, social, and physical elements of your life. A balanced person is a healthier leader.

God made us in His image, and He is the Creator. I believe that He is "well pleased" when we follow His example and work to create success in our endeavors. The entity that we lead having growth and success through

His blessing of our leadership will one day result in the coveted "Well done, thou good and faithful servant" (Matt. 25:21). It will be worth it all.

So if you are a leader, *lead*. Don't dictate. Don't drive people. Make sure you are with them and that they are with you. As one individual said to me: "If you get too far out in front of the troops, they will mistake you for the enemy!" And far too many leaders get killed by "friendly fire." Keep on keeping on with Jesus—He is our Creator, God, Savior, Leader, and our greatest example in leadership.

Chapter 14

THE RELATIONAL LEADER

David S. Penner

DIRECTOR, DOCTORAL LEADERSHIP PROGRAM,
LOMA LINDA UNIVERSITY SCHOOL OF PUBLIC HEALTH

Leadership seems to have fallen on hard times recently. While we see competition for the best places, we also observe many failed attempts, false starts, wrong moves, and embarrassing resignations. Weaknesses become readily visible and confessions public. Such a climate quickly leaves us confused. How should we relate to our leaders? Our feelings alternate between intrigue and disinterest. And those of us who ourselves are leaders are uncertain as how to proceed.

The confusion may arise, in part, from a wrong idea of what leaders really do. Society has convinced us that they are powerful, self-assured, and must always look the part. They must know all the answers and must always be right. Taking charge and driving change, they should accomplish great things and get good reviews and great ratings. Based on such a viewpoint, we have developed certain expectations for our leaders and, as leaders, have embraced them.

Such expectations are not new—they have existed throughout history. A few examples suffice. King Saul looked the part as he stood head and shoulders above others. Some noted that there was "none like him among all the people."[1] David received recognition even before he became king. Women sang and danced in his honor: "Saul hath slain his thousands, and David his ten thousands."[2] Nebuchadnezzar radiated confidence and self-assurance. He rose to prominence by his ability to get things done—in today's terms, by taking charge and driving change. He himself observed, "Is not this great Babylon, that I have built . . . by the might of my power, and for the honour of my majesty?"[3] Peter, self-assured and ready to lead the way, stepped out of the boat only to find himself deep in troubled water.[4] Whether ancient or modern, many leaders have tried to follow the same pattern.

Attempting to live up to such a model compels us to behave in awkward and inauthentic ways. It creates strained relationships with those we seek to serve. Even with the best of intentions and for honorable causes, we often find ourselves trapped in the default leadership style based on power and manipulation.[5] Problems arise. Although power attracts, it also drives others away. Pushback from colleagues and followers comes sooner or later. Receiving honor and glory is a heady experience, but the crowd tires easily. Since in this model failure is not acceptable, our constituents look quickly for another leader. Can we find a way to be authentic and avoid the temptation of power and control? What if our expectations and those around us were different? What if we conceived of leadership as serving others rather than demonstrating and maintaining personal power? What would leaders do in that setting?

We would certainly want to know what followers need and desire. In a recent seminar I asked the participants of several departments what they sought from their work (aside from a paycheck). The list was clear as they spoke genuinely of their needs. Several themes emerged. They wanted to be part of something important, something larger than their individual departments; to feel a sense of direction, purpose, and accomplishment; and to have a sense of belonging, security, and fellowship. In other words, they sought to be part of a community with a purpose. They desired interesting and challenging work and felt the need to be valued, recognized, and appreciated. Above all, they longed to serve and to help make a positive difference in the lives of those they encountered in the workplace, in the community, and in the larger world.

Here is a clear call for a quite different kind of leader-follower relationship. For those of us in leadership positions, it is actually very good news. No one is asking us to be or do the impossible. But neither does anyone want a top-down, power-and-control relationship that focuses its energy on compliance and conformity, forces others to blindly follow orders, and results in actions often described as "watching our back" and "covering our tail." The emphasis here is on a higher objective achieved through personal relationships. It concentrates not on ego building and perfect performance but on helping to find meaning, significance, and purpose. Everyone can get excited about such a goal.

In their book *Why Should Anyone Be Led by You?* two researchers from London Business School, Rob Goffee and Gareth Jones, asked what followers wanted from their leaders.[6] As was the case with my seminar group, they found that followers hoped for an authentic relationship. They sought: (a) *community* and a sense of belonging and feeling part of something bigger than themselves; (b) *authenticity*, that is, they choose to be led by humans, not titles or credentials; (c) *significance*, in that they wanted to believe that their efforts mattered; and (d) *excitement*, a spark to trigger their exceptional performance.

When we compare this to what leaders do, a pattern emerges. A quick review of current leadership literature reveals some interesting key points. Harvard professor John Kotter, in his seminal leadership article "What Leaders Really Do," refocused our attention on "setting direction," "aligning people," and "motivating and inspiring."[7] Peter Block identified the central task of leadership as building community, as he says, by "inviting conversation," "creating hospitable space," and "cultivating belonging."[8] David and Wendy Ulrich, in their bestselling book *The Why of Work*, described leadership as "making meaning in the workplace," "creating value," and "building hope for the future."[9]

When we step back from the need to be in charge, to look the part, or to feed our egos, we begin to see that what followers want and what leaders really do clusters in five significant areas. The common ground we seek with others is relational, that is, in finding *meaning, significance, community, direction,* and *excitement.*[10] Since leadership is relationship and relationship is two-way, tasks become mutual responsibilities common to everyone in the organization. Leadership does not rest alone on the shoulders of those in administrative positions. Because all participate in the responsibility, as leaders we don't demand the limelight but share it.

With the pressure on us now off, understanding replaces judgment, unity replaces the need for conformity, and commitment supersedes compliance. James Kouzes and Barry Posner report in their book *The Truth About Leadership* that in such a relationship people "feel empowered, listened to, understood, capable, important like they matter, [and] challenged to do more."[11] Once again, our organizations become a safe place that can encourage us to grow and develop in an environment free from embarrassment, harassment, physical and psychological harm, and the possibility of being taken advantage of by our leaders.[12]

Many biblical narratives illustrate relational leadership. Considering the setting, Abigail was an unlikely leader in a conflict between two powerful men.[13] But her story illustrates clearly the fact that leadership is not position but relationship. She stood between Nabal, her rude and demanding husband, and David, the powerful protector of the region who was also fired up with righteous indignation. Sensing the importance of the moment, she with courage sought resolution through kindness, humility, and truth. An essential characteristic of relational leadership is trust. Since members of her household felt safe sharing even sensitive things with her, it allowed her to respond quickly with bold action to avert wholesale loss of life.

Meeting David, she quickly gained his trust and respect. Her supreme act as authentic leader was the moment she spoke truth to power. Aggrieved, self-righteous, and incensed, David was bent on getting revenge. Choosing a humble yet courageous role, Abigail acknowledged the mistakes and at the same time sought to find meaning and purpose in the situation. Reminding David of the greater purpose that God had ordained for him, she pointed out the significance of his role, not only now as protector of those living on the frontier and the leader of his band of men, but also for the future, when he would be responsible for all of Israel. If he were to act within his right and use power, he would have blood on his hands, which would later reduce his influence as God's anointed king. David, to his credit, listened and accepted her counsel.

Her task only half done, Abigail then returned to Nabal, who ruled his household with his own might, made decisions with little regard to others, and always thought himself right and others wrong. In the end, he was unable or unwilling to hear Abigail and seems to have suffered a stroke when faced with the truth.

Moses in Egypt thought to drive change by his own power. As a result, he ended up with murder on his hands and a strained and awkward relationship with the very persons he wanted to help.[14] It took 40 years and several miracles, but he came back with a new focus, not on himself and his needs, but on God's purpose. This time he did not know the answers. In fact, God had to put words in his mouth and send Aaron along as translator. For the rest of his life Moses refocused his work on building community. He helped the Israelites to see the bigger picture and have hope for the future. They were to have purpose and to be part of something larger than themselves. Also he showed how on the personal level even the smallest acts could have significance and meaning.

Such examples urge us to think of leadership in terms of an empowering relationship. Just as current researchers note, leadership does not center on power and control, of having all the right answers, or of appearances. Pulling rank and making power plays is not leadership—it only serves to feeds our egos. We can see how David's intended actions, if he had followed through with them, would have bolstered his ego but at the same time led to serious loss of life and might have prevented him from leading Israel later as king. Nabal tried to take a shortcut to leadership. As with many other would-be dictators, his stubborn insistence that he was right and others wrong led directly to his demise.

Relational leadership has no shortcuts. Rather it is slow, repetitive, and at times seemingly unproductive. Moses experienced it as he led the children of Israel to the Promised Land. In this model one does not work for great rewards or glamorous moments. Significant moments, yes. Meaningful work, yes. Positive results, eventually. Further, Moses clearly demonstrated that relational leadership is not the gift of position or appointment but is something that we must earn. His inherited leadership position in Egypt turned out to be nothing. However, in the 40 years when he focused on bringing people together, he showed the lasting effects of relational leadership by creating *meaning, significance, community, direction, and excitement.*

Such examples allow us to see our role as leaders in a clear light and enable us to respond in authentic, God-centered ways. When we accept this, our new focus will be not on ourselves or our needs, but on others. And in so doing we will have found the heart of relational leadership.

---

[1] "When he [Saul] stood among the people, he was higher than any of the people from his shoulders and upward. Samuel said to all the people, 'See ye him whom the Lord hath chosen, that there is none like him among all the people?' And all the people shouted, and said, 'God save the king'" (1 Sam. 10:23, 24).

[2] "It came to pass as they came, when David was returned from the slaughter of the Philistines, that the women came out of all cities of Israel, singing and dancing, to meet king Saul, with tabrets, with joy, and with instruments of musick. And the women answered one another as they played, and said, 'Saul hath slain his thousands, and David his ten thousands'" (1 Sam. 18:6, 7).

[3] Nebuchadnezzar "walked in the palace of the kingdom of Babylon. The king spake, and said, 'Is this not this great Babylon, that I have built for the house of the kingdom by the might of my power, and for the honour of my majesty?' While the word was in the king's mouth, there fell a voice from heaven, saying, 'O king Nebuchadnezzar, to thee it is spoken; The kingdom is departed from thee'" (Dan. 4:29-31).

[4] "Jumping out of the boat, Peter walked on the water to Jesus. But when he looked down at the waves churning beneath his feet, he lost his nerve and started to sink" (Matt. 14:29, 30, Message).

[5] Simon Sinek explains how, when we do not know the *why* of what we do, we often knowingly or unknowingly resort to manipulation to get results. See Simon Sinek, *Start With Why* (New York: Portfolio, 2009), pp. 30ff.

[6] Rob Goffee and Gareth Jones, *Why Should Anyone Be Led by You?* (Boston: Harvard Business School Press, 2006), pp. 191ff.

[7] John Kotter, "What Leaders Really Do," *Harvard Business Review,* December 2001.

[8] Peter Block, *Community* (San Francisco: Berrett-Koehler Publishers, 2008).

[9] Dave Ulrich and Wendy Ulrich, *The Why of Work* (New York: McGraw-Hill, 2010).

[10] I presented an extended version of the five points at the American Health Care Congress, Dec. 7, 2010. A summary version appears in the November 2010 and February/March 2011 issues of the *Trans-European Division Leadership Development Newsletter.*

[11] James M. Kouzes and Barry Z. Posner, *The Truth About Leadership* (San Francisco: Jossey-Bass, 2010), p. 69.

[12] *Ibid.,* p. 78. "People won't take risks unless they feel safe. They need to feel secure that they will not be unfairly treated, embarrassed, harassed, harmed, or hurt when taking action."

[13] The story of Abigail, Nabal, and David appears in 1 Samuel 25.

[14] The morning after killing an Egyptian, the Israelite slaves, whom by his decisive action he had intended to help, questioned his leadership: "Who made thee a prince and a judge over us?" (see Ex. 2:11-14).

Chapter 15

The Humble Leader

Pardon Mwansa

Vice President, General Conference of Seventh-day Adventists

Dictionaries define humble as having or showing a modest or low estimate of one's own importance. That is, a person may have accomplished a lot or have a lot, but they don't feel it is necessary to advertise or brag about it. They refrain from making public or bringing into the limelight those accomplishments.

I once read a story that illustrates what it can mean to be humble. Soon after the renowned Black educator Booker T. Washington took over the presidency of Tuskegee Institute in Alabama, he was walking in an exclusive section of town when a wealthy White woman stopped him. Not knowing the famous Mr. Washington by sight, she asked if he would like to earn a few dollars by chopping wood for her. Because he had no pressing business at the moment, Professor Washington smiled, rolled up his sleeves, and proceeded to do the humble chore she had requested. When he was finished, he carried the logs into the house and stacked them by the fireplace. A little girl recognized him and later revealed his identity to the woman.

The next morning the embarrassed woman went to see Washington in his office at the Institute and apologized profusely.

"It's perfectly all right, madam," he replied. "Occasionally I enjoy a little manual labor. Besides, it's always a delight to do something for a friend." She shook his hand warmly and assured him that his meek and gracious attitude had endeared him and his work to her heart.

Humility is when you can, but you choose not to; when you are, and yet you don't proclaim it; when you can be listed, but you don't announce it. Or it is when you are very educated, very rich, in a high position in society, when everyone wants your signature, and yet you don't make a big thing out of all your success.

But humility is not easy even among believers or church leaders. The religious leaders of Jesus' time failed miserably on this point. Jesus warned people about how such individuals loved to walk around in "flowing robes and be greeted with respect in the marketplaces, and have the most important seats in the synagogues and the places of honor at banquets" (Mark 12:38, 39, NIV; see also Luke 11:43). And in His own teaching, being humble was so important that one day Jesus counseled, "When someone invites you to a wedding feast, do not take the place of honor, for a person more distinguished than you may have been invited. . . . But when you are invited, take the lowest place, so that when your host comes, he will say to you, 'Friend, move up to a better place.' Then you will be honored in the presence of all the other guests. For all those who exalt themselves will be humbled, and those who humble themselves will be exalted" (Luke 14:8-11, NIV).

What does the Bible teach about humbleness? Is humility an essential trait in the leaders God chooses to serve Him? If so, why? What do we learn from the life and leadership of Christ and from other great leaders in the Bible about humbleness in leaders? What happens to leaders who fail to remain humble? Are humble leaders born, or are they made? How is humility developed? How can we apply biblical counsel on humbleness to leadership today?

Humility Essential in Leadership

One of the qualities evident in those whom God has called to be leaders is humility. When God summoned Moses to leadership, the man's opinion and feeling about himself was that of inadequacy. "Who am I that I should go to Pharaoh and bring the Israelites out of Egypt?" was his initial response (Ex. 3:11, NIV). After God demonstrated some miracles aimed at convincing Moses that He would be with him and would enable him to succeed, Moses simply said, "Pardon your servant, Lord, I have never been eloquent, neither in the past nor since you have spoken to your servant. I am slow of speech and tongue" (Ex. 4:10, NIV) God made one more attempt by assuring Moses that He, God, had made the human mouth and would be able to help him. To this Moses responded, "Pardon your servant, Lord. Please send someone else" (verse 13, NIV). Moses was so humble that Scripture later describes him as "a very humble man, more humble than anyone else on the face of the earth" (Num. 12:3, NIV).

When Israel asked for a king and God consented to their request, the Lord chose Saul to be the nation's ruler. When God sent Samuel to anoint Saul as king, the prophet told him about God's plan. Saul's response was "But am I not a Benjamite, from the smallest tribe of Israel, and is not my clan the least of all the clans of the tribe of Benjamin? Why do you say such a thing to me?" (1 Sam. 9:21, NIV). So inadequate did Saul feel when called to leadership office that on the day of the public selection and inauguration of the new leader, he could not even make himself appear in public. When they looked for him, they could not find him. God had to reveal to the people where the man was, announcing that "he has hidden himself among the supplies" (1 Sam. 10:22, NIV).

The same feelings of inadequacy when called to leadership are what we find in Solomon and Jeremiah when they both exclaimed: "I am only a little child" (1 Kings 3:7, NIV; see Jer. 1:6, NIV).

The sense of insufficiency in those whom God calls has been a major factor to Him when He selects leaders, because when people feel inadequate about something, even though they may be quite competent, such individuals will depend on the Lord for their success. They have a sense of their dependency on Him that will make them successful in their leadership, because they will allow God to support them.

One of the reasons the Lord gave up on some of those He had called into leadership is that they ceased to be humble and became proud. No longer did they depend on Him as they led His people. Instead, they became proud of their own abilities, and that led to their downfall. As they stopped looking to God and His strength, they interpreted every victory that God gave them as evidence of their own abilities and the sole reason for their success. They put God out of the picture. As a result, victories become an opportunity for self-praise. Eventually God had no choice but to withdraw His power from them.

Why is God attracted to those who are humble when He is looking for a leader? Why does He have to desert those who become proud of their leadership? Constantly in Scripture God diminishes human ability so that men and women will depend on Him and not on themselves. Whenever people began to think that they could do something on their own, God allowed them to fail so that they would realize that only when He was helping them would they indeed succeed.

When it happened to Saul, the prophet Samuel reminded him, "Although you were once small in your own eyes, did you not become the head of the tribes of Israel? The Lord anointed you king over Israel" (1 Sam. 15:17, NIV).

When called to leadership office at the tender age of 16, Uzziah walked in the counsel of the Lord, and as long as he depended on God, the Lord gave him success. However, as Uzziah become successful, he became proud, and that pride resulted in his downfall. The Bible lists many great accomplishments by King Uzziah until his "fame spread far and wide, for he was greatly helped until he became powerful" (2 Chron. 26:15, NIV). Then Scripture says, "But after Uzziah became powerful, his pride led to his downfall. He was unfaithful to the Lord his God, and entered the temple of the Lord to burn incense on the altar of incense" (verse 16, NIV). No wonder the Bible says in Proverbs 11:2 that "when pride comes, then comes disgrace, but with humility comes wisdom" (NIV).

Jesus as a Humble Leader

What can we learn from the life of Jesus on being a humble leader? Philippians 2:1-11 invites us to have "the same mindset as Christ Jesus" (verse 5, NIV). Paul then explains what that attitude was when he says, "Who, being in very nature God, did not consider equality with God something to be used to his own advantage; rather, he made himself nothing by taking the very nature of a servant, being made in human likeness. And being found in appearance as a man he humbled himself and became obedient to death—even death on a cross!" (verses 6-8, NIV).

The apostle makes three important points to describe the characteristics of a humble leader, as exemplified by Jesus in this passage: The first point is in verse 3, where he says, "Do nothing out of selfish ambition or vain conceit. Rather in humility value others above yourselves" (NIV). It is not human or natural to consider others better than we are. Many times I have thought of what goes on in our minds during church elections, and how each of the potential candidates is likely to think of themselves as better than others. They hope to get elected to a position because they judge themselves as more qualified. This passage calls us to have a mind-set that regards others as better than ourselves!

The second point appears in verse 4 and builds on the first appeal: Each of you should look not only "to your own interests but . . . to the interests of the others" (NIV). A humble leader places not only their own concerns in their heart, but also those of others. They pray and work to make others successful.

The third point, in verses 5-8, is that you should "have the same mindset as Christ Jesus: who, being in very nature God, did not consider equality with God something to be used to his own advantage, rather, he made himself nothing, taking the very nature of a servant, being made in human likeness. And being found in appearance as a man, he humbled himself and became obedient to death—even death on a cross!" The attitude of such a leader reflects that of Jesus, who, although God, stooped down to be a human being and submitted to the lot of humanity. Jesus was God (John 1:1) and could command angels (Matt. 26:53). He did not have to be treated as a man or even be subjected to death. But even though He was in His very nature God, Jesus made Himself nothing. He took the nature of a servant and humbled Himself to become obedient even to the point of death—even the shameful execution on a Roman cross.

What Humbleness Is Not

We should never mistake weakness for humbleness, however. Being humble does not mean you keep quiet or allow other people to walk over you as a leader. During His life on earth Jesus one time drove people out of the Temple with a whip (John 2:13-16) and at another time told others, "Go tell that fox," referring to Herod the king (Luke 13:32, NIV). I guess what humility focuses on is doing things not for one's benefit but for the sake of others and the glory of God.

The Undergirding Principle for Humility

Is humility something we can all learn, or is it inborn in only some people? Can we develop it in our lives by the help of God? The Bible presents principles that if understood and practiced would enable anyone to be humble and remain that way.

James 1:17 teaches us what undergirds humility: "Every good and perfect gift is from above, coming down from the Father of the heavenly lights, who does not change like shifting shadows" (NIV). Such a recognition will lessen how much attention we pay to what we might have accomplished or have become. As a result, we will realize that whatever we have done or become has been God's gift to us. We will carry the attitude that was in

Nehemiah when he said, "The God of heaven will give us success" (Neh. 2:20, NIV). Deuteronomy 8:18 confirms this when it declares, "Remember the Lord your God, for it is he who gives you the ability to produce wealth, and so confirms his covenant, which he swore to your forefathers, as it is today" (NIV).

Humility is born or predicated on the premise that all good comes from God, and when we excel or are called to perform a duty, it is He who is accomplishing it through us. Hence all glory and honor is to go to Him.

It is the example that we find in Daniel, Joseph, Paul, and many other great leaders. Daniel found himself brought into the presence of the Babylonian ruler to interpret a dream. The king asked him, "Are you able to tell me what I saw in my dream and interpret it?" (Dan. 2:26, NIV). Daniel, who already had the knowledge of the dream, could easily have responded with a clear "Yes," but he did not. Instead he replied, "No wise man, enchanter, magician or diviner can explain to the king the mystery he has asked about, but there is a God in heaven who reveals mysteries. He has shown King Nebuchadnezzar what will happen in days to come" (verses 27, 28, NIV).

When summoned to explain a dream to Pharaoh, Joseph displayed a similar attitude. Pharaoh said to him, "I had a dream, and no one can interpret it. But I have heard it said of you that when you hear a dream you can interpret it." Humble Joseph replied, "I cannot do it, but God will give Pharaoh the answer he desires" (Gen. 41:15, 16, NIV).

In both cases the two leaders did not have to respond the way they did. They could easily have kept the role of God out of the picture and just said what He had revealed to them. But why did they say what they did? How important is what they said? I go back to the point that humbleness is a result of knowing and putting all that we are in its right place. I may have money, but who gave it to me? Who makes me still have that money? I may have intelligence, but who endowed me with it? Who makes me continue to have it? Our life is not in our full control. It is God who gives it to us all the time. All our abilities are not our own—they are a gift from God.

Examples of Humility From Great Leaders

Those credited with great leadership in the Bible have very little to praise about themselves. While standing in God's presence addressing Him, Abraham said of himself, "I have undertaken to speak to the Lord, I who am but dust and ashes" (Gen. 18:27, ESV). Paul spoke about himself as "the least of the apostles" (1 Cor. 15:9, ESV) and as the "very least of all the saints" (Eph. 3:8, ESV). David, at a time when he could have killed Saul but instead spared the king's life, referred to himself as a "a dead dog"; "a flea" (1 Sam. 24:14, ESV).

Conclusion and Application

The master leader, Jesus, was a humble leader. Those He called to guide His people were also humble leaders. God today invites us to have the same attitude that was in Christ Jesus. By His grace we too can be humble. How can we apply this matter to our day-to-day functions as leaders?

Presidents of conference do not cease to be one because they mingle with pastors, speak to "mere" laypeople, or are found helping in some duty. No one ceases to be college president because they took a ride in a bus or ate in the student cafeteria. I have seen this strange thing: leaders feel that by being too ordinary they cease to be effective. As a result, they choose to speak little and create an aura of mystery as a way of not being too common, lest they lose command. Some administrators cease to use the main door into the office because it is for commoners! One leader shared with me that he had stopped greeting the watchmen at his union office because it lowered his dignity. Becoming one among others in no way lessens or reduces a leader's effectiveness.

Nor do you have to keep people waiting on the phone or sitting for a while in the waiting room outside your office just to convince them that you are very important. They already know that, and that is probably why they are there to see you. People realize that you can influence others to hire them or even fire them. You do not have to remind them that you are the president.

Great leaders are humble, remain humble, and finish humble.

Chapter 16

THE COMPETENT LEADER

Gerry Karst

Vice President, General Conference of Seventh-day Adventists

What Does a Competent Leader Look Like?

Character.

The essence of who you are, is the result of daily, constant adherence to moral and worthy values. It is who you are when nobody else is around. Character defines the leader, and people are naturally drawn to those who have a moral character.

People follow a leader. Someone once said, "Stop and look behind you. If no one is following you, you are just out for a walk." Competent leaders inspire others to accept their direction and authority.

Personality.

It is what people see when they watch you. Do you radiate an inner happiness that makes others want to be around you? The personality of a competent leader gives evidence of positive thinking and acting. Such individuals think big, plan big, and expect big results.

Social skills.

Competent leaders can motivate people because they not only have a passion for the job but love those with whom they work. Such leaders have time for people, enjoy being around them, make others feel important, and are a joy themselves to be around. A good memory is useful, particularly when it involves those for whom you have responsibility. Remember the little things, such as names of family members and special days and events, and be ready to affirm and compliment others when they perform tasks well.

Vision: The Key to Leadership

No more powerful factor will drive any organization toward success and excellence than an attractive, worthwhile, and achievable vision of the future that those belonging to it widely share. That is the main message of leadership—everything else is a detail. But the secret of success in leadership is to be found in the details.

Vision is asking "Where are we going with this organization? What do we want it to look like in five or 10 years?" Quite simply, a vision is a realistic, credible, and attractive future for your organization. Since it always deals with the future, vision is where tomorrow begins. The Wright brothers did it when they dreamed of human beings flying in a machine. Henry Ford did it when he saw thousands of Americans motoring across the towns, cities, and country of America. Moses did it when he believed God's unimaginable future for an enslaved people. Nehemiah did it when he saw new and fortified walls around the ruined city of Jerusalem. And Jesus, from a cruel cross in old Jerusalem, had the vision of a lost people from a planet in rebellion becoming the redeemed in the New Jerusalem.

Because vision is central to leadership, one cannot lead without it. It is an indispensable tool for every organization and its members as they move into the future.

If you are the pastor or elder of a congregation, try this:

First, take an organizational picture of your congregation. For example, it will include the current membership, the current percentage of members returning a faithful tithe and giving offerings. It will capture the number of members involved in daily Bible study and personal prayer. And finally, it will look at what the congregation is currently doing in your community for outreach and mission.

Next, set some realistic goals for the future. In order to chart a new direction, you must:

Set forth a vision.

It should be so compelling that the majority will want to buy in and make it their own dream. But to accomplish that will require change. Recognize that such change is difficult for others to do and accomplish, however. It's the job of the leaders. For many it is a stressful process, and the leaders must be willing to take some measurable risks.

Communicate the vision.

Leaders need to be good spokespeople by using language that creates pictures in the minds of those they are guiding. If you are not inspired, your followers will not be either. Also understand that an important part of successful communication is to know how and when to listen.

Team Building

Jesus was the ultimate team builder. In Mark 2:14 we read, " 'Follow me,' Jesus told him, and Levi got up and followed him" (NIV).

A team builder needs to know how to *delegate* responsibility and how to *empower* people. What is the difference between the two words?

"Delegation" is the act of assigning work or responsibility to someone to carry out and fulfill a given task. "Empowerment" is the confidence and authority with which you invest a person to accomplish the task that you have delegated to them.

When choosing your team, look beneath the surface. Does the person possess values that will assist the team? In choosing a despised tax collector called Levi Matthew, Jesus went against conventional wisdom. Here Jesus taught us an important lesson. Our choices must rest on values and reflect much prayerful consideration. Do not surround yourself with only your friends or with people who think the same as you. A successful team needs the value of a contrary opinion.

By choosing Matthew, Jesus showed us that leaders should consider a diversity of people when creating a team. Don't make the mistake of picking those who look, think, and act alike. It was for the strength of the team that Jesus put a tax collector next to a fisherman, side by side in His training program.

Develop an inner circle. Jesus made every effort to give His 12 disciples close, concentrated attention, and at the same time He ministered to and fed the multitudes that sought to be with Him. However, some of Christ's most important lessons went to only Peter, James, and John. For those who find themselves chosen to lead, it is vitally important to their work and success that they have a special and close relationship with a small group of followers.

In the July 18, 2011, *Newsweek* Jack and Suzy Welch wrote an article entitled "How to Build a Winning Team." While addressed to corporate leaders who manage "for profit" companies, it recognizes four specific factors as essential for strong leadership teams. They can apply to church leadership as well, and I'm substituting "competent teams" for what the authors call "winning teams" in their magazine article.

The leaders of a competent team "always—always—let their people know where they stand."

Be direct, specific, and affirming of those who do well on your team. Sometimes individuals need to know that they should put their skills to better use elsewhere. One of the most challenging assignments leaders in church organizations have is that of reassigning low-performing individuals to areas where they can be productive. Because we are "brothers and sisters" who worship and socialize together, telling someone they need to be replaced is one of the most difficult tasks a leader can face.

Competent teams "know the game plan."

Explain your goals and procedures in clear, easy-to-understand terms that inspire enthusiasm and passion for the mission of the team.

Competent teams "are honest."

They don't reward mediocrity and don't play politics with the organization.

Competent teams "celebrate."

Acknowledge and honor small successes along the way. Such recognition encourages loyalty and stimulates creative thinking.

Effective and Productive Board Meetings

Recognize the Holy Spirit's involvement in decision-making.

Christian committees exist to find God's will. The Holy Spirit works through the people who make up the committees. Church committees operate on the premise that a Spirit-filled group makes more reliable decisions than just a Spirit-filled individual. "Let everyone be subject to the governing authorities, for there is no authority except that which God has established. The authorities that exist have been established by God. Consequently, whoever rebels against the authority is rebelling against what God has instituted, and those who do so will bring judgment on themselves" (Rom. 13:1, 2, NIV).

Focus on the mission of the organization.

Every effective organization must have a clear mission statement. Why does the institution exist? What are its goals and objectives? What does it expect to accomplish? A mission statement should be short, precise, and easy to remember. Members of the board should know and also be able to articulate the mission statement. One or two carefully constructed sentences should be enough to define the organization's reason for existence.

A barbershop had its mission statement posted on the wall. It went something like this: "The mission of this barbershop is to give patrons the highest quality haircut that results in an enjoyable and pleasant experience and for the lowest possible price."

Remember these six principles for Seventh-day Adventist boards.

1. The Lord ordained and built the organization. "Unless the Lord builds the house, they labor in vain who build it" (Ps. 127:1, NKJV).

2. We are presenting to our people the good news of the gospel. "Tell your children about it, let your children tell their children, and their children another generation" (Joel 1:3, NKJV).

3. As a board, we are the body of Christ. "As the body is one and has many members, but all the members of that one body, being many, are one body, so also is Christ. . . . There should be no schism in the body, but that the members should have the same care for one another. And if one member suffers, all the members suffer with it; or if one member is honored, all the members rejoice with it. Now you are the body of Christ, and members individually" (1 Cor. 12:12-27, NKJV).

4. Safety exists in boards. "Where there is no counsel, the people fall; but in the multitude of counselors there is safety" (Prov. 11:14, NKJV).

5. We are servant leaders. "Jesus called them to Himself and said to them, 'You know that those who are considered rulers over the Gentiles lord it over them, and their great ones exercise authority over them. Yet it shall not be so among you; but whoever desires to become great among you shall be your servant" (Mark 10:42, 43, NKJV).

6. We are God's partners and servants. "We are His workmanship,

created in Christ Jesus for good works" (Eph. 2:10, NKJV). "Even the Son of Man did not come to be served, but to serve, and to give His life a ransom for many" (Mark 10:45, NKJV).

The Work of the Chair

The most important part of the meeting is what happens before it begins. When you fail to prepare, you prepare to fail. Before the first participant enters the room, before the lights go on, before the meeting is even announced, come the critical steps of planning. They include: (1) determining the purpose of the meeting; (2) asking if the meeting is really necessary; (3) deciding what type of meeting it will be; and (4) building the agenda.

In developing the agenda, ask: 1. Can this item be resolved at the executive level? 2. Do we have enough information even to bring this item to the board? 3. Is the timing right for this agenda item? 4. Should this item be referred first to a small committee instead of the board?

Now you are ready to prepare the agenda.

The leader or chair should: (1) start on time; (2) restate the objective of the meeting; (3) stay with the agenda to keep the meeting flowing; (4) value the contrary opinion; (5) summarize comments; (6) remain neutral; and (7) end on time.

After the meeting, be sure to delegate responsibility to those who need to carry out the decisions. Evaluate the meeting's effectiveness and ensure that all board members receive copies of the minutes prepared by the board secretary.

How Does a Leader Become Competent?

Natural giftedness.

Some people are born with an aptitude for leadership. Early in life they show evidence of possessing its qualities.

Cultivated skills.

God helps equip leaders who are willing to learn. Many books, magazines, classes, and seminars teach leadership skills, and a competent leader will take advantage of the richness of resources available.

Learning from skilled leaders through observing them.
Watch those who have developed the art of competent leadership. Let their methods and practice guide the way you approach the responsibility.

Understanding servant leadership.
Remember that competent leadership in the church is a privilege and honor, not a right. God calls leaders in the remnant church to be servants and to remain humble in service.

Biblical Examples of Competent Leaders

Moses led a huge company of people, and he nearly worked himself to death until his father-in-law gave him some sound advice about delegating authority to others under his supervision. The Jethro principle of "small groups" is still valid today. By implementing Jethro's advice, Moses became one of the most "competent" leaders the world has ever seen.

Nehemiah is an outstanding example of competent leadership, as he demonstrated passion, inspiration, courage, and an unchanging focus on the mission before him. Study the book of Nehemiah as a manual for courageous servant leadership.

Jesus is the ultimate example of competent leadership. Carefully building an amazing team from disparate and varied personalities, He trained, encouraged, and modeled servant leadership in their presence, then made the ultimate sacrifice at the cross of Calvary. He loved the people He came to serve, and He knew what He needed to accomplish.

Chapter 17

THE LEADER'S PITFALLS AND SUCCESSES

Delbert Baker

VICE PRESIDENT, GENERAL CONFERENCE OF SEVENTH-DAY ADVENTISTS

Rains from Tropical Storm Agatha and natural conditions had apparently caused a sinkhole 100 feet deep and 65 feet wide in downtown Guatemala City on May 31, 2012. The massive sinkhole was so large that it entirely swallowed a three-story building. Onlookers said it was the most amazing sight they had ever seen. "The building was there one moment and gone the next!"

Closer examination, however, discovered that an earlier sinkhole had formed in the city back in 2007, killing three people. From a natural standpoint, sinkholes occur most commonly when groundwater or seepage from surface water sources dissolve underground layers of rock such as limestone. It creates large caves that eventually collapse. We know from this that sinkholes don't just happen. Rather, every sinkhole has a history.

A sinkhole or a pitfall is an analogy of what can happen in our lives and leadership when things go wrong. Encountering a pitfall is something that all leaders want to avoid. To successfully steer clear of them will take knowledge, intention, and personal initiative.

This chapter will define and explain leadership pitfalls and use the Bible and leadership literature to develop strategies to avoid them. An effective way to prevent such leadership disasters is to be forewarned and therefore to be forearmed (Matt. 7:24-27).

Ubiquitous Leadership

Leadership is everywhere. Everyone is a leader in some capacity, whether at work, at church, at home, or in the community. Such

119

responsibility deserves thought and strategy on how to best manage it.

Each person occupies a role in which they exert influence and have followers—thus they facilitate people to accomplish a desired goal. Peter intimated this when he wrote in 1 Peter 2:9, "You are a chosen generation, a royal priesthood, a holy nation, His own special people, that you may proclaim the praises of Him who called you out of darkness into His marvelous light" (NKJV).

Successful leaders work to have a better understanding of their own leadership personality and style. Furthermore, they nurture good leadership habits by having a principled leadership approach that ultimately prevents pitfalls because they have deliberately followed a careful course from the onset.

Ten principles particularly help strengthen and fortify leadership. The ever-improving leader:

(1) has a personal definition of what leadership is—achieves clarity.

(2) has a system for periodic self-evaluation—acts on feedback.

(3) does voluntary accountability checks—practices transparency.

(4) has a servant approach to leadership—cultivates humility.

(5) has a commitment to initiative—seeks improvement.

(6) schedules spiritual disciplines—nurtures Christlikeness.

(7) exemplifies key values—prioritizes God and family.

(8) engages emotional intelligence—manages emotions.

(9) has a positive forward view—envisions optimism.

(10) has a wholistic lifestyle—exemplifies health and wellness.

Good personal leadership practices act as an antidote to the dark side of leadership that trips up and sidetracks so many leaders.

Dark Side

The Bible contains a cadre of leaders who demonstrate the dark side of leadership, people who succumbed to the weakness of human nature and became victims of pitfalls.

In such biblical accounts we see Abraham's compromises, Jacob's manipulations, Aaron's vacillations, Moses' impatience, Balaam's greed, Samson's lusts, Saul's self-centeredness, David's adultery, Solomon's promiscuity, Nebuchadnezzar's grandiosity, Haman's cruelty, Caiaphas's expediency, Pilot's cowardice, Herod's pride, John Mark's timidity, and Demas' desertion.

In each case telltale signs beforehand indicated a weakness in the armor of the leader—one that, while understandable from a human standpoint, was preventable.

A perusal of leadership literature reveals a plethora of traits that have negative implications for leaders—traits that they should avoid. The following categories contain attitudes or actions that are either stand-alone leadership pitfalls or are leadership weaknesses that may lead to such a pitfall:

People habits:
> abusive, disrespectful, biased, hypocritical, insincere, insubordinate, intolerant, judgmental, revengeful, unethical

Principle traits:
> covetous, dishonest, ego-centered, immoral, foolish, promiscuous, selfish, spiritually insensitive, unjust, unprincipled

Practices:
> disingenuous, emotionally unintelligent, envious, inflexible, manipulative, noncommunicative, nonsupportive, pessimistic, unforgiving, vacillating

Productivity:
> arrogant, complacent, disorganized, incompetent, indecisive, intemperate, lazy, procrastinating, ruthless, shortsighted

Liability Asset Balance

Oscar Wilde is quoted as saying, "Experience is simply the name we give our mistakes." So while conventional wisdom bears out that all mistakes or pitfalls may not prove to be fatal and may provide learning opportunities, it's clearly much better to avoid the mishaps in the first place.

The liability asset balance (LAB) approach is helpful here. This approach states that when in professional and personal settings liabilities (shortcoming, foibles, or weaknesses) exceed assets (knowledge, abilities, skills, and talents) by too significant an amount or for too long a period of time, it offsets the balance (equilibrium or homeostasis), and the system will seek to self-correct or to restore that balance. In such imbalance, the system will either eliminate the person or at least try to correct the imbalance.

The LAB principle demonstrates that leadership is always on display. As Scripture indicates, where much is given, much is required (see Luke 12:48). Leadership is not about power, fame and fortune, or settling old scores. Rather, it involves truth and righteousness, service and commitment. It expects leaders to be ethical, impartial, and committed to the principles of justice and fairness.

Pitfall History

The story is all too common. A person has been a well-respected leader for years. Then, apparently without warning, he or she collapses into a sinkhole of shocking sin, calamity, and escalating revelations. Everyone wonders how a fall from grace could happen so suddenly. It soon becomes known that—like most sinkholes—it has a history.

Such incidents stem from a part of human nature—the sin problem. As long as we have earthly, sinful bodies we will have to be cautious about pitfalls (see Jer. 17:9). Paul was conscious of this when he expressed concern that after he had preached to others, he might become "a castaway" (1 Cor. 9:27). Expressing his self-distrust, he wrote: "I know that good itself does not dwell in me, that is, in my sinful nature. For I have the desire to do what is good, but I cannot carry it out. For I do not do the good I want to do, but the evil I do not want to do—this I keep on doing. Now if I do what I do not want to do, it is no longer I who do it, but it is sin living in me that does it" (Rom. 7:18-20, NIV).

Perspectives and Corrective

Rick Warren, of Saddleback Church in Lake Forest, California, lists several common church leadership mistakes that put individuals on the wrong path: You stop growing, stop caring, stop listening, get distracted, get complacent, become arrogant, and fail to delegate.

An insightful leadership research study conducted by John Zenger and Joseph Folkman and reported in their book *The Extraordinary Leader* (2009) identified five fatal flaws that represent behaviors and attitudes that will result in pitfalls for any leader who doesn't correct them. The research study conducted on 20,000 executives provides especially relevant information to the Christian leader.

The survey revealed that the core cause of fatal flaws was a fundamental lack of self-awareness and self-acceptance—ineffective leaders are not aware and/or they will not accept the reality of their flaws.

The five fatal flaw areas are intuitive and crucial:

1. **Inability to learn from mistakes:** The research indicates that derailed executives made about the same number of mistakes as those whose careers progressed, but they did not use their setbacks or failures as learning experiences. As a result, they continued to repeat the same type of mistakes.
   Corrective: Profit from feedback and learn from mistakes.

2. **Lack of core interpersonal skills and competencies:** Regardless of how smart you are or how effective your combination of intelligence, hard work, managerial acumen, and administrative skills may be, nothing can take the place of emotional intelligence or core interpersonal skills. The saying goes that "we hire people for their technical competence and fire them for their interpersonal incompetence."
   Corrective: Always be in a mode to use and increase your emotional intelligence.

3. **Lack of openness to new or different ideas:** This flaw is a game stopper. It demoralizes subordinates and frustrates upper management because it keeps conditions in a form of lockdown. People feel unappreciated, fresh ideas get ignored, and it discourages change.
   Corrective: Be open to new ideas and ways of doing things.

4. **Lack of accountability:** Without accountability leaders often set the standard high for everyone but themselves. Adverse to accepting responsibility, they will go to great lengths to shift the blame for shortcomings, yet they will claim credit for progress.
   Corrective: Accept responsibility for your portfolio areas, buffer your subordinates, and praise others for a job well done. Put the well-being of others and your organization before your own.

5. **Lack of initiative:** Here leaders simply follow the letter of their

job description and fail to prepare for challenges and future needs. Always waiting to see what is going to happen before they move, they are cautious to a fault. To them it is all about protecting themselves and doing little that will threaten their sense of security and entitlement.

Corrective: Keep asking such questions as: How can we better prepare for the future and better facilitate goals? Then promptly act to make it happen.

Paths to Progress

The pressing question naturally follows: can leadership flaws be corrected? The answer is that it depends. The ability to self-correct depends on four critical factors—all of which must be present:

1. **Personal openness:** The leader must be willing and able to acknowledge and accept critical feedback from those around them.
2. **Personal patience:** The leader must be committed to putting forth the effort to make the necessary changes.
3. **Organizational supportiveness:** The organization or supervising persons must be willing to give individuals a chance to correct their leadership style and not harbor negative or accusatory feelings toward them, but offer them a real opportunity to succeed.
4. **Organizational understanding:** The organization's leadership must be willing to allow sufficient time for the leader with the flaw to make the necessary changes. Key persons must remember that it is impossible for the process to be a perfect linear upward progression.

Pitfall Recovery

After a leader has fallen into a sinkhole, how do they get out? Zenger and Folkman found that while most executives have the capacity to make the necessary changes, the real question is whether they have the stamina and will to work consistently and diligently to make the necessary transformation. It reminds us of the question that Christ asked the sick man at the Pool of Bethesda: "Do you want to get well?" (see John 5:1-8). For astute leaders, recognition that their choices created the problem is the first step toward resolving it. Then the leaders must make a determined commitment to implement the necessary changes—regardless of the consequences.

According to research, it takes between six and 18 months for a leader to correct leadership flaws that led to a pitfall—and that's assuming that the individual is exhibiting only one flaw! If the person has more than one flaw, in a combination of two or more, the prospects for a successful recovery become increasingly difficult.

Personal and spiritual self-examination is critical to the recovery process (see Ps. 26:2 and 1 Cor. 11:28) and includes hard soul searching for what went wrong and what must be done to make it right and prevent it from happening again. Ellen White gently urges, "Now let every person search his own heart and plead for the bright beams of the Sun of Righteousness to expel all spiritual darkness and cleanse from defilement."*

Restitution, support, and accountability are important factors at this point. However, one thing is clear: leaders who experience a pitfall must not stay there. They must take decisive action to get out of the sinkhole. It requires fixed determination, and they must keep in mind that in order to claw their way out of some sinkholes they may have to ask for assistance (see Phil. 4:13; Eph. 6:10-18; Ps. 103:1-5).

Conclusion

Portia Nelson wrote what she called "Autobiography in Five Short Chapters."

Chapter 1

I walk down the street. There is a deep hole in the sidewalk. I fall in. I am lost . . . I am helpless. It isn't my fault. It takes me forever to find a way out.

Chapter 2

I walk down the same street. There is a deep hole in the sidewalk. I pretend I don't see it. I fall in again. I can't believe I am in the same place, but it isn't my fault. It still takes a long time to get out.

Chapter 3

I walk down the same street. There is a deep hole in the sidewalk. I see it is there. I still fall in . . . it's a habit. My eyes are open. I know where I am. It is my fault. I get out immediately.

Chapter 4

I walk down the same street. There is a deep hole in the sidewalk. I walk around it.

Chapter 5

I walk down another street.

The application should be clear to the leader who is ever improving. Pitfalls may happen, but they are costly. Climbing out of one takes great effort. Most are preventable, but in every case, regardless of conditions, the leader's choices and resolve make the difference.

---

* E. G. White, *The Adventist Home*, p. 549.

Sources

Anderson, Dave. *How to Lead by the Book*. Hoboken, N.J.: John Wiley & Sons, Inc., 2011.

Bruner, Pamela, and Jack Canfield. *Tapping Into Ultimate Success*. Carlsbad, Calif.: Hay House, 2012.

Chamine, Shirzad. *Positive Intelligence*. Austin, Tex.: Greenleaf Book Group Press, 2012.

Damazio, Frank. *The Making of a Leader*. Portland, Oreg.: City Bible Publishing, 1988.

George, Jim. *A Leader After God's Own Heart*. Eugene, Oreg.: Harvest House, 2012.

Nelson, Portia. *There's a Hole in My Sidewalk*. Hillsboro, Oreg.: Beyond Words, 2012.

Sanders, Oswald J. *Spiritual Leadership*. Chicago: Moody Press, 1994.

Zenger, John, and Joseph Folkman. *The Extraordinary Leader: Turning Good Managers Into Great Leaders*. Columbus, Ohio: McGraw-Hill Co., 2009.

Chapter 18

The Leader and Failure

Derek J. Morris

Editor, Ministry Magazine

The pages of Scripture contain numerous stories of leaders who failed. At times the accounts are painfully explicit—even embarrassing. Consider the Old Testament story of King David's moral failure: covetousness, abuse of power, adultery, deception, and murder. Many wonder why the Inspired Record includes such graphic details. In the New Testament we find more narratives of dismal failure. Matthew records the account of one of the closest disciples of Jesus who not only failed to speak up for his Master during His trial but also denied Him with lies and curses. And then we find reports of corporate failure—wayward generations, immoral churches, and dysfunctional families.

Why does the Bible report such incidents of failure? What vital lessons can we learn for our lives today?

Let's begin with the assertion that failure is a painful part of life on our damaged planet. No one is immune from it. No wonder the apostle Paul admonishes the members of a broken congregation in Corinth: "Let him who thinks he stands take heed lest he fall" (1 Cor. 10:12, NKJV). How then shall we live?

Since failure is a real possibility, have a strategy in place to avert it before it happens. A classic example is the story of Joseph. The young Hebrew slave was a victim of sexual harassment. Unfortunately, he was not free to leave and had no legal rights. His owner's wife came to him repeatedly with a bold and blatant proposition: "Lie with me" (Gen. 39:7, 10, NKJV). Finally, with careful scheming, she crafted her promiscuous plan. Having made arrangements for all of the other servants to be outside the house, Potiphar's wife threw herself at Joseph and seized his garment. With no time to work out a plan, no opportunity for rational dialogue,

Joseph needed to act promptly. His commitment was already clear and settled: "How then can I do this great wickedness, and sin against God?" (verse 9, NKJV). Joseph's strategy was also in place: run. Although he could not run far, he could still remove himself from the compromising situation.

The biography of Joseph reminds us that we do not always get immediately rewarded for seeking to honor God and do what is right. However, the rest of the story confirms the promise of the Lord recorded by the psalmist Asaph: "Call upon Me in the day of trouble; I will deliver you and you shall glorify Me" (Ps. 50:15, NKJV).

Unfortunately, not all failures get averted. As a young pastor, I heard the story of a colleague who jested that a church member was flirting with him. "Don't worry," he said. "I can handle it." Such naive self-confidence is careless and delusional. Within two weeks he handed in his resignation. That pastor should have recognized that failure was a real possibility and implemented a strategy to prevent it before it occurred.

Recently my wife told me the story of another pastor summoned late at night by a single woman "in need of pastoral care." Wisely, that pastor took his wife with him. When the church member opened the door, her provocative attire exposed her inappropriate intentions. The pastor and his wife were shocked but not ruined.

The apostle Peter, who experienced painful failure as a result of careless self-confidence, gives us a solemn warning: "Be sober, be vigilant; because your adversary the devil walks about like a roaring lion, seeking whom he may devour. Resist him, steadfast in the faith, knowing that the same sufferings are experienced by your brotherhood in the world" (1 Peter 5:8, 9, NKJV).

Even though failure is a real possibility, you don't need to live your life in fear. Having counseled us to take heed lest we fall, the apostle Paul then shares this good news: "No temptation has overtaken you except such as is common to man; but God is faithful, who will not allow you to be tempted beyond what you are able, but with the temptation will also make the way of escape, that you may be able to bear it" (1 Cor. 10:13, NKJV).

A wise leader implements strategies to block failure before it happens. But what should you do if it does occur? Be honest. Admit your wrongdoing to God and to those affected by it. After reading the account of King David's dismal moral fall, many wonder that Scripture would refer to him as a man after God's own heart (see Acts 13:22). Perhaps that character description had in mind earlier days when David did walk in the way of the

Lord. But it's also possible that he demonstrated himself to be "a man after God's own heart" by the way he handled himself in the midst of failure. Listen to his testimony recorded in a psalm of repentance: "Create in me a clean heart, O God, and renew a steadfast spirit within me" (Ps. 51:10, NKJV). David knew well the negative consequences of self-deception and denial during a time of failure: "When I kept silent, my bones grew old through my groaning all the day long. For day and night Your hand was heavy upon me; my vitality was turned into the drought of summer" (Ps. 32:3, 4, NKJV). He also knew the joy that comes when we admit our failure to God and accept His forgiveness: "Blessed is he whose transgression is forgiven, whose sin is covered." "I acknowledged my sin to You, and my iniquity I have not hidden. I said, 'I will confess my transgressions to the Lord,' and You forgave the iniquity of my sin" (verses 1, 5, NKJV). Every leader's life will have times when they will need to pray, "Create in me a clean heart, O God."

Wintley Phipps tells the story of his interaction with President Bill Clinton during the Monica Lewinsky scandal. The Lord impressed Phipps to send Clinton a message: "Mr. President, read Psalm 69." Sometime later Phipps was attending a function at the White House, and one of the president's Cabinet members called him aside and said, "You don't know what happened, do you? The president read that psalm. He called a few of his closest Cabinet members together and shared with us from Psalm 69." In that psalm David admits his failure to God: "O God, You know my foolishness; and my sins are not hidden from You" (verse 5, NKJV). Having read that inspired account of how to handle failure, President Clinton went to his room and wrote out the first speech that he gave to the American people admitting that he had sinned. Phipps was asked to be in the audience at the White House when the president gave that speech.

Many people have judged President Clinton for his foolishness. Why didn't he have a strategy in place to avert such failure? To those accusers, Jesus might say, "Let the one who is without sin among you cast the first stone" (see John 8:7) and "Judge not. . . . How can you say to your brother, 'Let me remove the speck from your eye'; and look, a plank is in your own eye?" (Matt. 7:1-3, NKJV). All of us have experienced times of failure. If you fail, don't lie, make excuses, or try to cover up. Admit your sin to God and to those it has wronged. Humble yourself under the mighty hand of God. Ask for forgiveness and cleansing. We all can give thanks to God for the promise that "if we confess our sins, He is faithful and just to forgive us our sins and to cleanse us from all unrighteousness" (1 John 1:9, NKJV).

God not only longs to forgive you and cleanse you if you fail, He also wants to teach you valuable lessons in the midst of your failure. He longs for you to learn through your experience and avoid needless repetition of the same mistakes. In the same scripture song in which David exposes the futility of self-deception and denial in the midst of failure, he also recognizes God's desire to teach us valuable lessons for the future. Under the inspiration of the Holy Spirit the psalmist cites the words of the Lord: "I will instruct you and teach you in the way you should go; I will guide you with My eye" (Ps. 32:8, NKJV). What warning did God long to offer to David that balmy evening just before he took a stroll on the roof garden of his palace? What counsel did He desire to give to an adulterer that might have avoided the senseless murder of a faithful and loyal soldier? God seeks to teach each one of us valuable lessons in our times of failure.

Think about your life. Consider those times when you have had either personal or professional failure. What counsel did God desire to share with you that might have prevented such heartache and pain? The Lord appealed to David and also to us when He urged: "Do not be like the horse or like the mule, which have no understanding, which must be harnessed with bit and bridle, else they will not come near you" (verse 9, NKJV). While failure is a painful reality in our broken world, you don't have to stumble from one disaster to another. God will teach you. He will counsel you.

One vital lesson that God wants to teach each one of us is the need for compassion when dealing with others who have failed. In reference to Peter's behavior during the trial of Jesus, Ellen White writes, "The Savior's manner of dealing with Peter had a lesson for him and for his brethren. It taught them to meet the transgressor with patience, sympathy, and forgiving love. Although Peter had denied his Lord, the love which Jesus bore him never faltered. Just such love should the undershepherd feel for the sheep and lambs committed to his care. Remembering his own weakness and failure, Peter was to deal with his flock as tenderly as Christ had dealt with him."* The person who has been forgiven much will love much (see Luke 7:47).

Failure is part of the present life, but through the enabling presence of the Holy Spirit such times can become opportunities for grace and growth. We don't have to pitch our tent in the midst of failure. Instead, we can choose to move onward and upward. No wonder Jude concluded his brief inspired epistle with these words: "Now to Him who is able to keep you from stumbling, and to present you faultless before the presence of His glory with exceeding joy, to God our Savior, who alone is wise, be glory and majesty, dominion and power, both now and forever. Amen" (Jude 25, NKJV).

---

* E. G. White, *The Desire of Ages,* p. 815.

Chapter 19

The Accountable Leader

Ivan Leigh Warden
Associate Director, Ellen G. White Estate

onsidered by many as one of the best leaders to have ever lived,
Aristotle once stated, "We are what we repeatedly do. Excellence, then,
is not an act, but a habit." According to *Webster's New College Dictionary*,
"excellence" is "the fact or condition of excelling; superiority; surpassing
goodness, merit, etc.; something in which a person or thing excels;
particular virtue." Leaders come in all shapes, colors, and genders. There
are "born leaders" who have such charisma that people instinctively follow
them. "Institutional leaders" acquire their influence from their place in
a company, a college, a community, or a nation. "Bestowed leaders" gain
their significance by virtue of position or job title.

To be a leader there must be followers. Without followers you will not
have leaders. You will find leaders in academia, the field of business, even
in gangs and prisons. From the White House to the city hall and from the
military to the farm you will encounter leaders everywhere.

A fundamental assumption that many hold is that leaders have
certain characteristics, traits, and attitudes that cause people to follow
them. One such characteristic is listening: the leader who has excellence
as a modus operandi will have developed the art of active listening. Aly
Wassil, in his book *The Wisdom of Christ*, states that "the art of listening
requires concentration, reflection, and meditation, where upon follows
illumination."[1] Additional traits include intelligence, self-confidence,
determination, integrity, sociability, skill in planning, and the ability to
execute the plan, to name a few. Different situations demand different kinds
of leadership. No single leadership style will be effective in all contexts.
One situation will bring forth one kind of leader while other circumstances
will cause a different person to be a leader.

Just as leadership is tough to get a handle on, so is excellence. What is excellence in one situation may not be so in another. Alfred Lansing's book *Endurance: Shackleton's Incredible Voyage* is a classic. It portrays how one leader demonstrated excellence.

South Pole explorer Ernest Shackleton planned to cross on foot the last uncharted continent. His ship the *Endurance* set sail from England in August 1914. In January 1915, after battling its way for six weeks through 1,000 miles of pack ice and now only a day's sail short of its destination, the vessel became locked inside an island of ice. Then for 10 months it drifted northwest before the ice finally crushed it. But the ordeal had barely begun for Shackleton and his crew of 27 men. It would end only after a near-miraculous journey by him and a skeleton crew through more than 850 miles of the South Atlantic's roughest seas to the closest outpost of civilization. The survival by Shackleton and all 27 of his men for more than a year, as *Time* magazine put it, "defined heroism."

His experience is an example of excellence—the leaders' standard.

The leader who strives to achieve and maintain excellence should be guided by this quote: "Good, better, best, never let them rest, until your good is better and your better is best." Perfect performance comes from perfecting practice. While it is an awesome challenge to reach excellence and win a championship, it is even more so to maintain that level at all times. Aristotle was truly correct when he stated that "excellence is not an act but a habit." One must truly commit everything in the daily strive for excellence.

If you look at sports as an example, winning a championship is an immense challenge, but gaining a second or third one is a herculean task. Implementation of the "good, better, best" quote does not allow for a lackadaisical spirit or mediocre approach.

How does an individual or team know when they have reached the level of "best"? It is not always easy to identify. However, it is a great benefit if those who are already champions are there to coach the player or the team. Having already attained a level of excellence, they can pass on necessary factors to enable the team to achieve its goal, objective, or dream. Bill Russell's name, for example, has gained fame as a leader in the National Basketball Association and the NBA franchise of the Boston Celtics, whose standard was (and still remains today) excellence. Russell won 11 NBA championships as a player and player coach.

Look around, whether in the past or today, and you will find leaders and excellence coming together in the fields of science, art, literature, mathematics, business, education, religion, media (social, print, and screen), politics, the military—and the list goes on. Sad to say, some never achieve the level of excellence that was right within their reach—theirs for the taking. Something impedes their progress. But what is it?

We must beware of the little thief that distracts us from reaching our goal of excellence. Called procrastination, it puts off until tomorrow what needs to be done today. Procrastination says, "Not this morning, but perhaps tonight; not now, but later." This thief will pick your pockets and take your valuables, but you will not immediately miss what it has stolen from you if you are not daily in excellence mode. If we are to truly excel, like our Master, our Lord and Savior Jesus Christ, we must say no to the procrastination thief so that we can stay on the road that leads us to "good, better, best."

My model of leadership and excellence is Jesus. He has always existed with God the Father, and He is the Creator. John 1 tells us the Word became flesh and dwelt among us. The omnipotent, omniscient, omnipresent, immutable God came to earth to live and die so that we might have eternal life. Notice how Ellen G. White described it:

"The world was made by Him, 'and without Him was not anything made that was made' (John 1:3). If Christ made all things, He existed before all things. The words spoken in regard to this are so decisive that no one need be left in doubt. Christ was God essentially, and in the highest sense, He was with God from all eternity, God over all, blessed forevermore."[2]

Jesus came to our sinful world to be our excellent leader. He is the only excellent sacrifice to die on our behalf on the cross at Calvary, then to rise from the grave and give us, His followers, a ticket beyond death and the grave. Not only did He teach us how to live in this world—He also showed us how to be leaders of excellence. Thus He is our paradigm, or example. When we are born again, the Savior of the world gives us His will and strength and a new value system (see John 3). His grace and mercy allow us to become leaders of excellence. The excellent leader, by doing and praying each day, will grow in grace and mercy (see Eph. 2:8), being strengthened to continue to press for still more excellence.

Jesus, the daily-wage carpenter, excelled in His human father's shop. In the classroom He was an excellent teacher and leader—from telling parables to opening a supermarket in the desert and feeding thousands. Always He was the consummate leader in excellence. No matter what your socioeconomic status in this life, no matter what your zip code may be, no matter your IQ, you can reach lofty heights. You can, by His grace and mercy, accomplish "good, better, best." Never forget what Paul penned in Philippians 4:13: "I can do all things through Christ which strengtheneth me."

I challenge you to continuously press onward toward the mark of excellence, making it your standard as a leader.

---

[1] Aly Wassil, *The Wisdom of Christ* (New York: Harper and Row, 1965), p. 113.
[2] E. G. White, *Selected Messages,* book 1, p. 247.

Chapter 20

Legacy: What Leaders Leave

Charles E. Bradford
*Retired Pastor, Evangelist, Department Director,
Conference President, and General Conference Officer*

A faithful, sensible servant is one to whom the master can give the
responsibility of managing his other household servants and feeding
them. If the master returns and finds that the servant has done a good job,
there will be a reward. I tell you the truth, the master will put that servant
in charge of all he owns. But what if the servant is evil and thinks, 'My
master won't be back for a while,' and he begins beating the other servants,
partying, and getting drunk? The master will return unannounced and
unexpected, and he will cut the servant to pieces and assign him a place
with the hypocrites. In that place there will be weeping and gnashing of
teeth" (Matt. 24:45-51, NLT).

Every believer has a legacy, a sacred trust to use for building up the
body of Christ, to fulfill its mission—the proclamation of the final message
of mercy to a doomed planet. Not restricted to ministers or church officers,
that mission involves the whole people of God. The Lord is an equal
opportunity employer. The entire believing community is responsible for
completing that mission. We are richly endowed because Christ has made
us "depositaries of most precious doctrines . . . unmixed with errors and
traditions of men."[1] Christ "has promised power to every soul who works
in faith and love and truth, believing the promise."[2]

Most leaders worry about their legacy—that is, "What will people
be saying about me when I am no longer around? How will history treat
me?" The people whom God assigns for His service also wonder about
their legacy, but not for the same reasons. Their concern is, "Is my service
pleasing to my Master?" The good servants know exactly what the Master
requires of them—that they must care for others. "Feeding and leading"

is the way some express it. You will notice the servants take care of others before themselves. They must be unselfish. Also they must be aware of the Master's return. Forgetfulness is inexcusable, because it leads to bad behavior.

Jesus warned against inactivity—laziness. During the interval between His ascension and return the servants must keep busy. Educators talk about employing time "on task." What we do must not just be busywork but intelligent ministry. And we must not forget that all we do must stem from love.

"There was once a man descended from a royal house who needed to make a long trip back to headquarters to get authorization for his rule and then return. But first he called ten servants together, gave them each a sum of money, and instructed them, 'Operate with this until I return'" (Luke 19:12, 13, Message).

Forgetting self and losing oneself in the service of others develops nobility of character. It leaves no time for navel gazing, daydreaming, and narcissism. Former enemies of God—that's what we were, members of a planet in rebellion—under the new situation now become officers of the court with subpoenas and general amnesties for all who will submit to the risen Lord.

And all this happens "until I return"! Scholars tell us that the inference here is that as soon as Jesus left He was already on His way back. You see, He really loves those former rebels and wants very much for them to be where He is.

Ellen White puts it powerfully: "It would be well if those occupying positions of trust in our institutions would remember that they are to be representatives of Jesus. True goodness, holiness, love, compassion for tempted souls must be revealed in their lives. Christ gave Himself to the world, that He might save those who would believe in Him. Shall not we, partakers of this great salvation, value the souls for whom He gave His life! Let us labor with a perseverance and energy proportionate to the value Christ places upon His blood-bought heritage. Human souls have cost too much to be trifled with, or treated with harshness or indifference."[3]

As such servants we make a difference—we add spice to life, a pleasant aroma, "a savour of life unto life" (2 Cor. 2:16). That is what God had in mind when He said to Moses, "I will take some of the power of the Spirit that is on you and put it on them" (Num. 11:17, NIV).

What we desperately need is a renewed focus on the church as God's agency for salvation. Its members are ambassadors and peacemakers—which brings us to the central idea of the question of legacy. Leaders can only leave what they have—that is, themselves. True leaders give themselves away. They infuse their followers with the spirit that energized and motivated them—to be kind, generous, and helpful to all, especially those in their charge. This transfer from leader to people is real—from the one who serves to the ones being served. In the economy of salvation nothing is lost. Every good deed is somehow preserved. "We may never know until the judgment the influence of a kind, considerate course of action to the inconsistent, the unreasonable, and unworthy."[4] Others may forget what we say—our preaching and lectures—but they will never forget how we treated them, whether we came across as phony or real. They are reading us all the time. Acts of kindness and deeds of love are absolutely immortal. They do not just vanish from the earth.

So the kind of leaders we are talking about are in themselves a gift—to associates, family, community, church, fellow travelers. And the gift keeps on giving. Even the account of our deeds may spur someone on to serve others. And the gift still keeps on giving. Monuments, statues, plaques, will "dim and lose their value," but a little pebble cast into the sea of human need makes ripples and sometimes waves far beyond our little service area.

"So let's not allow ourselves to get fatigued doing good. At the right time we will harvest a good crop if we don't give up, or quit. Right now, therefore, every time we get the chance, let us work for the benefit of all, starting with the people closest to us in the community of faith" (Gal. 6:9, Message). No matter what our rank or station, as we give of our best we contribute to the building up of the whole people of God. Heaven cannot overlook this. Angels record every effort.

Leaders are talent scouts who recognize in others the gifts that God has granted and their commitment to service. Then true leaders will transmit their knowledge and vision to them. "In their turn [they] transmit the precious legacy of truth, pure and uncorrupted, to others." "We want every responsible man to drop responsibilities upon others."[5]

To us has been given the precious legacy of Christ's teaching. The only begotten Son of God was nailed to the cross of Calvary that He might bequeath to the fallen race a legacy of pardon.

The harvest is coming when we shall reap what we have sown. There will be no failure in the crop. But now is the sowing time. Now we must make efforts to be rich in good works, "ready to distribute, willing to communicate" (1 Tim. 6:18), laying up in store for ourselves a "good foundation against the time to come," that we "may lay hold on eternal life" (verse 19).

People are our legacy, the fruit of our labors in Christ. Redeemed by His blood, they will go on throughout eternity. The apostle states it clearly: "You yourselves are all the endorsement we need. Your very lives are a letter that anyone can read by just looking at you. Christ himself wrote it—not with ink, but with God's living Spirit; not chiseled into stone, but carved into human lives—and we publish it" (2 Cor. 3:2, 3, Message).

A day will come when it all will be revealed—the rest of the story. The ultimate experience takes place on that sea of glass shot through with fire when someone picks you out of the crowd, runs to greet you, and says with deep emotion, "It is because of you that I am here."

This is the legacy, the gift that keeps on giving. "Men and women who have lived wisely and well will shine brilliantly, like the cloudless, star-strewn night skies. And those who put others on the right path to life will glow like stars forever" (Dan. 12:3, Message).

---

[1] Ellen G. White, in *Signs of the Times,* Nov. 16, 1891.

[2] Ellen G. White, in *Gospel Herald,* Mar. 1, 1904.

[3] Ellen G. White, *Christian Leadership* (Washington, D.C.: Ellen G. White Estate, 1985), pp. 7, 8.

[4] *Ibid.,* p. 7.

[5] E. G. White, *Testimonies to Ministers,* pp. 302, 303.

A Call to Action

Ministry to the Cities
Ellen G. White

This compilation is a call to action—a plea for believers to work for their Savior by bringing the gospel to the millions of people crowded in the cities of the world. Topics include the challenges of ministering in the city, strategies, methods, selecting and training workers, and lessons from Scripture.

It's time to go downtown and get busy.
978-0-8280-2665-9

Availability subject to change.

The Blueprint
Rico Hill and Jared Thurmon

How can we reach the teeming multitudes in our cities with the gospel? You can find an answer in *The Blueprint: A Manual for Reaching the Cities*. Rico Hill and Jared Thurmon present the Beehive method, a tried-and-true approach to urban ministry with a new twist. Based on the methods of Jesus and an intriguing dream of Ellen White's, they describe a model that they have successfully tested in modern urban outreach. 978-0-8280-2714-4

Empowered
by Truth

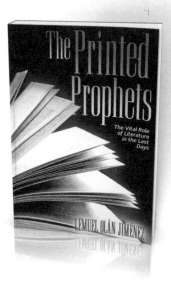

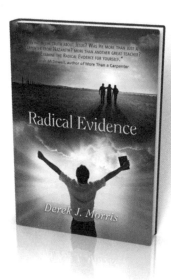

The Printed Prophets
Lemuel Olán Jiménez

In these days of earth's final crisis, God has designed that literature will serve as printed "prophets" announcing future events, as "preachers" drawing our attention to the Lord's soon return, and as "messengers" declaring God's great love and mercy.

The Printed Prophets, by Lemuel Olán Jiménez, explores why literature will be so critical in end-time evangelism and how you can help fulfill prophecy by sharing it.
978-0-8280-2703-8

Radical Evidence
Derek J. Morris

Derek Morris introduces you to people who have had a dramatic encounter with the Messiah they honestly didn't believe existed. There is a Shiite Muslim, an African ancestor worshipper, and others.

Take a look at the evidence, and see if God is showing His face to you.

Hardcover: 978-0-8127-0514-0

DVD Series: Four presentations: each approx. 28 minutes. 978-1-936929-07-8

"Train up a child . . ."

Yeah, but how?

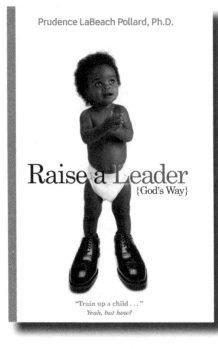

Raise a Leader eBOOK AVAILABLE
Prudence LaBeach Pollard, Ph.D.

We want our children to grow into godly leaders who will guide and direct others in the Christian life. But how do we help that happen?

Prudence LaBeach Pollard draws on years of study to provide encouragement—and biblical guidance—on such subjects as parental responsibility, defining boundaries, genuine self-esteem, and character development.

We all have ambitions for our children. Here's hope that you can raise and nurture your children to become all that God designed them to be. 978-0-8280-2636-9

Availability subject to change.

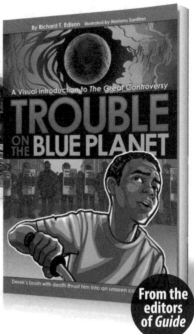

This Could Change Everything

Find transforming power for your life

Do you feel like temptations always beat you into submission? You can't seem to win a victory and wonder if you're not trying hard enough, or if God isn't holding up His end of the bargain.

In the book, *Transformation*, Jim Ayer opens up about his own experience as a serial sinner and tells how he connected with the power that God has provided to change us from the inside out.

A companion study guide, *Your Daily Journey to Transformation*, Jim and Janene Ayer take individuals or small groups on a 12-week journey toward a transformed life—a life shaped and energized by the Holy Spirit.

"Behold, I make all things new," says Jesus. See that promise fulfilled in your life today. Paperback, 978-0-8280-2711-3

Your Daily Journey to Transformation
A 12-week Study Guide
Paperback
978-0-8280-2702-1

Availability subject to change.